HIDDEN HEROES

LIGHTS IN A
DARK PLACE

True Stories of God at Work

in Colombia

WHAT CHILDREN ARE SAYING ABOUT HIDDEN HEROES

"This is my favorite Christian book!"

"I'm thinking of being a missionary myself!"

"This is probably the best missionary story I've heard."

"I love your books! They're really good!"

"You've really taught me a lot with these books!"

"It's perfect."

"The chapters all have great names!"

"These are the best books ever!"

"I love your book please write more books I love them!"

"I have learned to be a better testimony!"

"I want to hear more!"

HIDDEN HEROES SERIES

LIGHTS IN A DARK PLACE

True Stories of God at Work

in Colombia

REBECCA DAVIS

CF4·K

10 9 8 7 6 5 4 3 2 1
© Copyright 2014 Rebecca Davis
ISBN: 978-1-78191-409-0

Published in 2014
by
Christian Focus Publications,
Geanies House, Fearn, Tain,
Ross-shire, IV20 1TW,
Great Britain

Cover design by Daniel van Straaten
Cover illustration by Del Thompson
Other illustrations by Del Thompson
Printed and bound by Nørhaven, Denmark

Contents

To Russell Stendal and all the Stendal family.
You and the many other missionaries of Colombia have been an
inspiration to me.

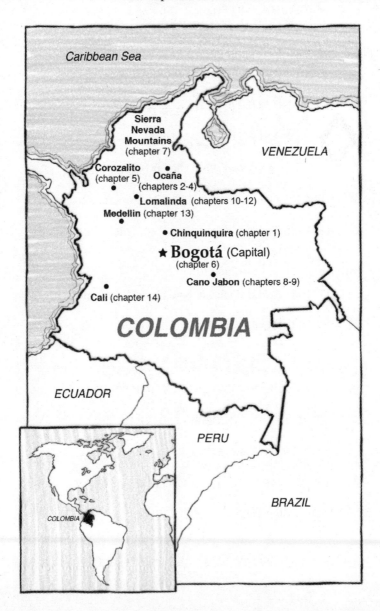

1. LET'S GET STARTED

One Colombian man spat right in the face of John Harbeson. "Who are you, you crazies? You want to give me that devil trash?" He took the Bible and threw it down and ground his foot into it.

"The priest said you're from the devil!" another man yelled. "You don't honor the Virgin!" He threw a rotten tomato at Jack Thomas. Then another.

"Ha! Ha! Look at those gringos!" The whole crowd jeered and pointed. "Those evangélicos!"

It was 1935. John and Jack had come to Colombia to bring the gospel of Jesus Christ to a land whose people saw themselves as Christians. But the Colombians feared the Bible—the priest told them it was dangerous to read it—so they had no idea what it said. They were told that the evangélicos were from Satan.

"We'd better get away and pray, brother," whispered John.

"Right," Jack answered. They dodged the crowd to head back to their small room to spend time before the

Lord. "We trust You, Lord," they prayed. "We're not afraid. We pray for the people of Colombia, that You will open their blind eyes to Your great love through Jesus Christ."

Back they went. This time, when they offered the Bibles, they did it quietly, almost secretly. One person after another, with a fearful look, sneaked up to them to say, "I want one. Don't tell anybody."

"Father in heaven," John and Jack prayed, "our goal is to see a church here, in this city. One true church, O Lord, filled with believers."

John, his new wife Rachel, and Jack kept on speaking and continued to hand out Bibles and booklets. Several years passed and finally the mayor said, "We've watched you all this time, and we know you're from God, with the true message for Colombia. You can visit the jail and tell your message there. Maybe it will help those murderers and cattle thieves."

John visited the jail every Sunday. "What have these men been jailed for?" he asked.

"Oh, murder, mostly," said the jailer. "Murderers get three years. Some of them are in for stealing cattle."

Every Sunday, John preached in the jail and handed out New Testaments and small booklets. "You've been told that you must work your way to God," he said.

"That's a hopeless way. However, this holy book tells us that there is only one way to God, and that the true way is through faith in Jesus Christ."

The murderers and cattle thieves were enthusiastic and took the little books and Bibles. But the jailer listened too.

"This is the true way," he said. "I know I can't work my way to God. I know I have to trust in Jesus Christ alone. I've got to tell my sisters."

The jailer's two sisters worked in the cathedral. When their brother came to get them, they eagerly joined the little meeting in the prison. "We could hear you preaching in the street!" they told John. "Every time you preached, we were listening behind the window curtains in the cathedral! We've listened to you for over a year. We knew you spoke truth, but we were afraid. Now we're not afraid any more."

"We've always known the Bible is a holy book," said the jailer. "But we've also been told that it's a dangerous book and that if we misread it, it will send our souls to hell. Some people ... well ... are confused and think it's evil. Sometimes the priests even say that. I think they're afraid of it."

"We've never had a Bible," said one of the sisters, "so we didn't know what it said. Now that we do, we want you to show us where it says Jesus is the only way."

John turned to John 14:6 and showed them. "Jesus said, 'I am the Way, and the Truth, and the Life. No one comes to the Father, except through Me.'"

The sister nodded. "Jesus is the only way," she said. "It says so right there in the Holy Bible. Is there any place in the Bible that says we should come to God through the Virgin?"

"No," said John. "It's not there."

The other sister sighed. "So much time wasted in blindness," she said. "I'll need to read the whole thing myself, just to be sure."

Someone else came to the jailer and said, "Did you know that the priest has put you out of the church? He excommunicated you because you no longer adore the holy Virgin, and because you read that book when he told everybody not to."

Excommunication was the most terrible thing that could happen to a Roman Catholic. They were told that it meant they would go to hell—there was no hope for the salvation of their souls. One of the sisters put her head right down on the shoulder of the other and began to sob.

"Don't cry, sister," John said, trying to encourage her. "Your hope isn't in the priest, or the Catholic church. It's in Jesus."

She looked up. "Do you think I weep for my own soul?" she cried. "No! I weep for those wicked priests who have deceived us all these years!"

* * *

John, Jack, and Rachel were some of the first missionaries in the country of Colombia. But years before, others had gone ahead of them, passing out Scriptures, portions of Scriptures, and little books; all at the risk of their lives.

In 1939, another missionary, Elof Anderson, knocked on the door of a house in a small village. Elof was used to being cursed, beaten, and chased out of the town. But he knew that in every place, God had His people.

A Colombian man opened the door, looked at him, then looked at the Bible he held, and said, "When is the meeting?"

"Uh … what are you talking about?" Elof stammered.

"You have a Bible there, don't you?" the man asked. "Are you an evangélico?"

"Yes," Elof answered. "And I have some other—"

"Come in, come in!" said the man. "I've prayed for forty years for you to come!"

"Forty years?" said Elof. "How?"

The man walked to a trunk and pulled out a big Bible, old and worn.

"I got this forty years ago from an American who came up this trail from the city." I've read it and read it so many times, I've memorized it. I know it's true, but I don't understand it all. I've prayed for forty years for God to send me someone to teach me.

"Now, you've come! My family and neighbors will listen, so let's get started."

* * *

Elof Anderson gave the gospel of Jesus Christ to that man, and others around him, who came to Christ. Here and there, small churches began to form, like fireflies of light around the nation of Colombia.

See Thinking Further for Chapter 1 on page 135.

2. ROSA AND THE CHRIST STATUE

Rosa Franco prayed with her eyes open, and her face up. "If you'll heal my little boy, I'll make an offering to you every week for a year." She prayed to the huge bronze statue that stood outside of Ocaña, almost hovering over the whole town.

It was 1948, and the Christ statue, El Cristo Rey, had stood there for thirteen years. It stood as tall as three men, on top of a pedestal twice that high. With its huge bronze arms outstretched, it looked as if it could do anything.

"I'll keep this vow!" Rosa cried to the statue. "Every week I'll bring you an offering, even if it means I go hungry! Just heal my little boy!"

Rosa trudged back down from the statue to Ocaña with a heavy heart. Little Santander, her son, had only recently started to walk. She had seen at birth that one of his feet was twisted, but now she could see how that twisted foot affected him. Even though he was almost two, he hobbled, turning his foot to one side and walking on his ankle. Bruises and sores covered the area of his feet which he tried to walk on.

"I have faith," Rosa muttered as she trudged. "I have faith in El Cristo Rey. Surely if I give a good offering, he will hear my prayer." Women in the village who were older and wiser than her had assured her that if she made a vow and kept it, then ... well ... maybe ... El Cristo Rey would heal her son.

Week after week, Rosa trudged up to the plateau where El Cristo Rey stood. Week after week, she prayed. But little Santander's foot remained the same. His twisted ankle was still covered with bruises and sores from his hobbling. Santander's father, Marco, seemed too busy with his store and his farm to pay much attention to the little boy. The other children, all older, ignored him as they worked and played. Rosa shed secret tears.

One day, two teenage cousins, Carlos and José, came to visit from a leprosy colony where they lived because of their father's disease. They wandered about the store with Rosa and Marco, glancing at this and that.

"What's this?" asked Carlos, suddenly curious. He pointed to a small booklet inside a glass case.

"Oh," Marco answered, embarrassed. "It's just a paper from those wicked evangélicos. It's full of lies."

Carlos reached for the paper and studied the front. "Four Things God Wants You to Know."

Marco waved his arm, as if he wanted to wave away his embarrassment. "Every pair of shoes I bought from that shoemaker, every pair had one of those things in it. He's a good man, an honest man. I don't know why he would do such a thing. Maybe somebody else did it when he wasn't looking."

Carlos asked casually, "Have you read it?"

"I'm sure whatever it is, it's evil heresy," Rosa answered. "But you know we can't read."

"It's not evil, Aunt Rosa," said José. "It's about God's love."

God's love? Surely it was some kind of false teaching. "You boys learned to read?" Marco asked.

"Yes, we learned in the leprosy colony. That's where we learned about God's love, too, and we have a book even better than this one. It talks about good news." Carlos pulled out a black book from his bag, found his place, and began to read.

"Shepherds were in the fields watching over their sheep. And suddenly, the angel of the Lord came over them, and God's glory shone around them. And they were very frightened."

Marco's face settled into a relaxed smile. This was a familiar story, the Christmas story. There would be no *evangélico* false teaching in this. "Come, children," he called. "Listen to Carlos read this story." From different parts of the store and from outside, the five children gathered. Little Santander obediently hobbled to stand next to his mother.

Carlos continued. "And the angel said to them, 'Don't be afraid, because I bring you good news of great joy, for all people. Today, in David's city, is born for you a Savior, Christ the Lord.' "

Marco nodded and smiled. Every good Catholic should know this story.

But José spoke up, boldly. "There's another word for 'good news,' " he said.

Everyone listened.

"It's ... it's ... *evangelio*."

Rosa gasped. *How could this be?*

The children drew back. The evangelio was wicked! Everyone knew that. The priest, the old people, all of them talked about the evil activities of the evangélicos and their wicked doctrine. Some people even whispered that they sacrificed children!

Marco's eyes clouded over with darkness. "What is this book you're reading from?"

"It's the Holy Bible, Uncle Marco," Carlos answered meekly.

Marco's face showed his confusion. The Holy Bible? "Well ... well ... I don't see anything evil in it."

"This is a true book, isn't it, Uncle?" asked José.

"Yes, yes, of course. It's the Holy Bible." Marco had never seen one before and didn't know what was in it, but he knew it was a book to be honored.

José turned to Antonio, the oldest son. "Did you hear what the angels said?"

"Yes," answered Antonio. "They brought the good news—the evangelio—that the Savior was born." Again, the others gasped. Antonio had used that word!

"Uncle," José continued with determination, "who did they say would be the Savior?"

17

"Well, Christ the Lord, of course." Marco snapped out the words.

"Yes, sir. When you truly believe that in your heart, and truly trust Christ the Lord as your own Savior, then you're an evangélico."

For a minute, no one spoke. Everyone was stunned. They had never heard anything like this before.

José and Carlos waited for the words to sink in. "This is truly good news," José pressed on. "Our heavenly Father offers forgiveness of sins through Jesus Christ."

Suddenly a new realization dawned before Marco's eyes. "Are *you* an evangélico?"

"Yes, Uncle Marco." Both boys answered at the same time, quietly but firmly.

Alicia, the oldest girl gasped again. "I can't believe it," she murmured. "In our own family!"

None of them had ever even seen an evangélico, at least not that they were aware of. They had only heard about them. These kind, polite boys who carried Holy Bibles and that honest, hard-working shoemaker just didn't fit the description of evangélicos that the Franco family had heard about.

Even so ... the warnings, the descriptions, the priest's curses, those all won out over the kind spirits of the young men who sat before them. Marco turned, without another word, and stomped out of the store. Some of the children followed him.

Hesitantly, the two boys turned to their aunt and tried again. "Listen, Aunt Rosa. Do you want to hear the words of Jesus? Do you believe He spoke the truth?"

How could she answer? The words of Jesus—there was no way they could be false. Rosa slowly nodded. Had she ever even heard the words of Jesus?

"This is what Jesus said," Carlos read. " 'Truly I say to you, the one who listens to my words and trusts in the one who sent me, has everlasting life. He will not go into judgment, but is passed from death to life.' Jesus rose from the dead. All who trust in Him will rise from the dead with Him."

"There would be no purgatory, then?" Rosa asked tentatively.

"No, Aunt. There is no purgatory in the Holy Bible. If you trust in Jesus alone, you're safe in Him."

What strange words! What new words, frightening, but hopeful! Rosa asked question after question. The boys answered by reading to her from the Bible.

Suddenly, Rosa sat up straight. She remembered something.

"I've made a vow to El Cristo Rey. I have to keep that vow." Somehow she knew that this vow, that statue, didn't match with these new words.

19

"You don't have to keep the vow, Aunt Rosa."

"No, I must! You don't understand! It's for the healing of my child's foot!" She pointed to Santander, who played on the floor not far away. His twisted foot turned in an odd direction, covered with sores and bruises.

"Aunt Rosa." José spoke in frustration. "That old statue is nothing but cold metal. It can't do anything for Santander."

The words struck like an arrow into her heart. This very thought had continued to prickle inside her mind every time she made the long trip with her offering. She had pushed it away day after day.

"Aunt Rosa," Carlos continued with more calmness. "The living Christ can do this. He can heal Santander. Trust Him." Then he began to read from the Holy Bible again, stories of the miracles of Jesus, the loving touch of Jesus, the healing care of Jesus, the true Jesus; not a metal statue. Rosa closed her eyes and leaned back in her chair. Tears began to flow down her cheeks. She had never heard any words so beautiful.

After the boys had gone back home to the leprosy colony, Rosa's heart was in a turmoil. Could she believe in this evangelio way? What would it mean for her? What would it mean for her family? What would it mean for her vow, and little Santander?

20

Rosa continued to make her pilgrimages to El Cristo Rey. One time she even took Santander with her. With her little boy squirming in her arms, she knelt before the cold, hard metal statue. She looked up at the cold, hard bronze arms and the cold, empty eyes. How could she have thought they looked compassionate?

She left her offering in the basket and carried her little boy away, her heart heavy, as if it might break under the weight of the cold, hard bronze.

If her son were to be healed, would it be El Cristo Rey who healed him, that cold hard figure? Or would it be the *living* Christ? With trembling, Rosa finally decided to no longer pay her vow to the statue.

"Living Christ, living Christ," she prayed silently. "If You heal my son, I will become an evangélica, even if … even if … ." She couldn't finish the sentence. What would it mean to become an evangélica? What kind of life would it be? Everyone she knew hated them with a terrible hatred. That included Marco, the father of all her children. "If You show me this great mercy, how can I do any less than give my life to You completely?"

Rosa kept her prayer a secret. With their busy family life, no one noticed that she no longer made the long treks out to El Cristo Rey. Marco paid no attention to their little son.

Rosa watched and prayed.

And watched.

And prayed.

Then, she saw it, and she knew. Nobody else noticed, but she did.

She had to speak out. *But what would her family say?* She had to speak out! *But what would Marco do?*

Months passed. By the time their nephews came to visit again with their Bibles, Rosa was ready.

"Look, everyone!" she cried out. She held up her little boy's foot, now straightened. "The living Christ did this! The living Christ! He healed Santander's foot! He answers prayer! The evangélico way is the way of truth!"

* * *

At first, Marco Franco was furious with Rosa because she had become one of the hated evangélicos. For a long time, he resisted Jesus Christ, the true and living way. But eventually he, along with Rosa and their entire family, became passionate evangélicos. They loved their many enemies and preached the good news of complete salvation in Jesus Christ.

See Thinking Further for Chapter 2 on page 135.

3. MARCO AND THE BURNING HOUSE

Marco Franco stumbled headlong into his house. Behind him, he pulled his new friend, the traveling pastor and teacher Vicente Gómez. He slammed the door just in time, against the pounding and the yelling.

"We'll get you, you evangélicos! We're not finished with you!"

But marvelously, the attackers moved back from the house.

"Oh, Marco, I thought you were a dead man!" Rosa sobbed. All the children stood around her, crying just as loudly. The little ones ran to their daddy and to Pastor Vicente.

"Oh, Rosa," Marco gasped. "Our good Father preserved us from that insane mob. Careful, don't hug me too hard. Oooh!" He grimaced and groaned, pulling back his shirt to reveal huge red welts on his back from the lashes he and his friend had just received from the mob. Gingerly, he fingered his red and purple face where they had punched him again and again.

"If they'd broken any bones," Vicente murmured, holding his head, "if they'd broken our legs ... there would have been no way we could have escaped. They would have beaten us to death."

"Why can't you protect yourself?" Rosa cried out through her tears. "Why do you have to just take it? I saw you almost grab that pole and start to swing it at them! But then you stopped. Is this what a loving Father wants? Does He want us to just stand by and take these attacks? What if you had been killed?"

"But I wasn't killed," Marco answered quietly. "I don't know what came over me, thinking I should have wielded that pole. That's why I dropped it. You saw." Marco shook his head slowly. Somehow, just for a moment, he had reacted with all the quick rage and violence of his life before he came to Christ.

"Yes, I saw from your face that you knew you shouldn't fight back. Nevertheless, can we never fight back?"

"Rosa, weren't you praying?" Vicente asked.

"Well, yes, sort of," she responded almost helplessly. "Mostly I just screamed and cried."

"Prayer is our way of fighting back," Vicente continued. "Prayer, and love. Loving our enemies is more powerful than any physical weapon."

"We'll keep on with our house meetings, Rosa!" Marco said. "More and more people come to them. They come because they're curious about our apparent lies, but they stay because they hear the truth! They know that this terrible violence all over Colombia grows worse. That means we should have more meetings, not fewer. If they're all going to die, they need to first have a chance to hear the good news of the great salvation of Jesus Christ."

One day when Marco went to town to buy supplies, he was late coming back. A man ran to give Rosa a message. "Rosa, come to town!" he said. "There's something wrong with Marco."

Rosa's heart leaped into her throat, and her stomach lurched. *Oh no, Father, did they attack him again? Is he going to die?*

In town she found her husband on a bed, feverish, calling for her, his pale face white like death.

"It was the police," he said weakly. "They beat me and beat me. Just because I'm an evangélico and hold meetings in my home."

Rosa got Marco home, where she and the children nursed him back to health. But even after he was better physically, Marco didn't get up from the bed. He didn't want to pray. He turned his face to the wall, and often, Rosa caught sight of secret tears flowing down his cheeks. He was a man who never cried, a man who was always bold. Why did Marco cry secret tears? He lay in bed, asked his family to leave him alone, and cried. He couldn't bear to hear them sing.

What's wrong with him? Rosa wrung her hands in prayer. *Father in heaven, what's wrong with him?*

Finally, Vicente Gómez, the traveling pastor, was able to visit. "Oh, Don Vicente." Rosa almost choked on her words. "His body is better. However, there's something wrong in his spirit. I don't know what it is!"

Vicente went to the bed where Marco lay. "Jesus understands your pain, my brother," he said. "It was the officers of the law that beat Him too."

Marco groaned and lifted his hand to hide his face. "I was beaten like Jesus," he moaned. "Yet I am not like Him in any other way. I'm probably not even a true Christ-follower."

Vicente and Rosa exchanged troubled glances. "What do you mean, brother? Do you want to go back to your old way of life?"

"No, that's not it," Marco groaned. "I've seen my heart." He began to weep, and couldn't speak for a minute. "I'm not like Jesus," he moaned. "I don't love my enemies. Over and over, I think about those policemen who beat me. If I had a machete or a gun, I know what I might have done to them. I imagine all the violence of my old days, raging against my attackers." He caught his breath for a moment and couldn't speak. Then he choked out, "Don Vicente, every time I ask Jesus to forgive me for these thoughts, and then, just as soon as I receive forgiveness, they all charge back, and I go through it all again. I have no victory. Only defeat. I am no evangélico." He turned his face back to the wall, and his shoulders began to shake.

Don Vicente gently placed his hand over Marco's hand. "This has been too much for you to bear," he said. "I know what we should do. We'll cancel all future meetings here at your house. Then you'll be safe."

Suddenly Marco turned back to stare at Vicente in shock. "What are you talking about?" he said. "These people who come here, lots of them aren't evangélicos yet. They need Jesus. They need the Way, the Truth, and the Life. Think what will happen to them if they die before they hear."

"What if some of them report you to the police again?" said Vicente. "Aren't they your enemies too?"

"What are you talking about?" Marco's voice came back in strength. "I've never heard you talk like this. Rosa!"

"Yes, Marco?" his wife answered anxiously.

"Get me my pants and shirt! Get me my shoes!" He sat up and reached out his arm impatiently.

With a slight smile and a twinkle in his eye, Vicente asked, "Whose side are you on?"

"The side of the evangelio," Marco growled. He suddenly realized what Vicente had done, and his voice came even stronger. "The side of Jesus Christ."

Vicente gently patted his friend's back. "It's no sin to be tempted, Marco," he said. "It's sin only when we welcome the temptation."

For the first time in weeks Marco sat up at the church meeting in his home. He sang with his brothers and sisters in Christ and listened to Vicente preach. "If a grain of wheat doesn't fall into the ground and die, it abides alone. Yet if it dies, it will bring forth much fruit. He that loves his life shall lose it, and he that hates his life in this world will keep it, to life eternal" (John 12:24).

"Rosa," Marco whispered later that night. "It's gone. I don't feel it any more. No more desire for vengeance. No more hatred. If I had a chance, I would tell all those policemen of the love and joy of Jesus Christ. If they beat me, I know that Marco Franco can't love them. But Jesus Christ in me loves them, and He never stops."

What kind of faith is this that won't fight back?

In some of the people of Ocaña, Marco's gentle reaction of love sparked a greater rage than ever.

28

The police were violent men who had been taken out of the prisons and given uniforms, and they relished the thought of further destruction. When the Catholic priest gave them the word to destroy that entire family of evangélicos, they jumped at the chance.

One night, in the middle of the night, a drunken mob came up the road. Too late Marco and Rosa Franco awoke, too late they grabbed their little ones from sleep. The house had been set on fire.

When they tried to run out, a drunken man slashed a machete toward them. "Oh no, you don't!" he yelled. "Get back in there, cursed evangélicos, or we'll shoot you all! We have the house surrounded!" Yelling out their hatred, the crowd shouted until their throats became hoarse, until their voices were drowned out by the roar of the fire.

Rosa and Marco stood inside the burning house with their seven children, crying out to God to rescue them. *Would these people really commit such a terrible crime?* The flames leaped higher, and the heat began to become almost unbearable. The children screamed.

Finally, little Emelina, six years old, ran to the back door with determination. She was small enough, she reasoned, that she could dodge through the legs of the violent crowd, and then she could run fast out into the woods.

When she jerked open the back door, no one was there. "Mamá!" she cried. "They're gone! They're gone!" Her voice barely carried over the roar of the fire.

With the babies in their arms and holding the little ones' hands, Rosa and Marco ran to the door. All nine of them ran and ran, right out into woods. Only then, in the safety of the dark trees, did they turn to peek out from behind bushes to see what had happened. They peered past the eerie yellow raging glow of the crackling fire, to see the glow on the other side reflected from many faces.

The drunken mob no longer surrounded the house, but they hadn't really left. The heat of the fire had caused them all to retreat to the road, where they all still stood silent, watching as if in a trance. The bizarre shadows cast by the writhing flames had hid the shadowy figures of nine people who ran out the back and into the safety of the woods.

The crowd no longer heard any screams from inside, only the roar of the blaze. Then, moments later, the fire caught a gasoline tank. The entire house exploded.

One by one, silently, the drunken crowd dispersed. They had done what they came to do, or so they thought. Would they be able to sleep without nightmares that night?

Through the night, the Franco family huddled in the woods, whispering, trembling. "Thank You, our mighty Deliverer. You rescued us. We praise You." They watched the fire continue to burn down until the entire house was only charred rubble.

Days later, when the family was finally able to meet with Pastor Vicente again, Marco beamed with joy. "I

know I've lost everything," he said. "You remember last month, how broken in spirit I was because I couldn't love the people who persecuted me? Look at what the living Christ has done now! My soul is enriched with the love and forgiveness of Jesus! Do you think Marco Franco could do this? Oh, no, Marco Franco could never do this. This love that I feel for my enemies, this is what Jesus Christ has done in me."

Quavering whispers passed from one house to another. "Did you hear? Did you hear? Did you hear that the Franco family escaped the fire?"

"Escaped!" Shocked whispers spread throughout the community and, like the waves of a pebble cast into the water, spread into all the communities around. "Impossible! They were driven back with machetes and guns! The house blew up!"

"No, they escaped. *All of them,* even the little ones. They've left the village, but they haven't stopped being evangélicos. They've gone to live someplace else, but they're as bold in their speech as ever. They even talk about *loving their persecutors.*"

Fear struck one household after another. This was too powerful a love. Guilt raged through the hearts of some of the men who had lit the torches.

What kind of faith is this, that won't fight back? What kind of religion is this, that is so full of love and forgiveness?

With the Franco family gone, one secret believer after another in Santa Inés and the surrounding area publicly announced his faith. "I am an evangélico. I believe that salvation is not through the Virgin or through my prayers or the Mass, but only through Jesus Christ. I will offer that faith to others. I'll host the church meetings in my home."

More and more new congregations arose throughout the region. Around the house that stood blackened, charred, and utterly destroyed with all the Franco family's belongings, here and there in the mountains and the valleys, new families declared their faith in Jesus Christ. More curious listeners came to hear the powerful words of life from the Holy Bible. "Truly I say to you, the one who listens to my words and trusts in the One who sent Me, has everlasting life. He will not go into judgment, but is passed from death to life."

This was a sure faith for which the new evangélicos would willingly suffer. The kindled fire of the good news of Jesus Christ casts sparks of light from the Franco home in every direction, to one village after another.

See Thinking Further for Chapter 3 on page 136.

4. JOSÉ AND THE DEMONS

He had always wanted power. Wealth, honor, and great power. That was what he wanted. That's why José Pinzon decided to become a priest. He hid his dagger near the shrine so it could soak up some special powers so he would never need to be afraid.

But now … he had just heard some news that he could hardly believe. *Did the priest really plot to murder people?* That wasn't what a priest was supposed to do!

José left Catholicism. He studied other religions. He studied communism. He still wanted to find power, real power.

Then, somehow, he found a book that told him how he could gain power from Satan, unimagined power and riches. He could call up the very presence of Satan himself.

José closed himself up secretly in his small room. His fingers trembled and his breath came in short gasps as he began to follow every detail of the instructions. Hour after hour passed as he lit candles and muttered secret words and made motions with his arms. His eyes began to glaze over.

Then, suddenly, José became aware of a terrifying presence in his room. Darkness surrounded him, darker than anything he had ever known. Terrible, unearthly sounds filled his ears.

José screamed. "Am I in hell?" He threw the book across the room and jumped up and ran out the door, breathing heavily, his bloodshot eyes wide with terror.

Had he sold his soul to the devil? Could he escape from that evil presence?

Terrified, José put the evil book in a box and piled stacks of other books on top of it and hid it under his bed. But night after night, he couldn't sleep. He tossed and turned, filled with terror of the evil presence he had called into his life. He began to drink more and more strong drink in order to try to forget the frightening evil presence in his room. He began to feel terror of the judgment of the holy God.

José's sister wanted to help him. She went all the way to Ocaña to get a sacred heart of Jesus for him, but when she came back, the sacred heart had broken apart. It was hollow inside.

"How can this thing help me?" José cried out. "The presence of evil was very real, but this sacred heart of Jesus is just fake. How can I get help?"

José stood alone on a mountain ridge. "God in heaven!" he cried out. "Everything about You that I've seen is false, and yet I fear Your judgment!" He covered his face with his hands, and began to shake with tears.

One day, at the coffee plantation where he worked, José saw a man who held a small black book. Somehow he felt strangely drawn to that book, yet at the same time strangely repelled by it.

"You're one of those evangélicos, aren't you?" he said.

The man nodded.

"I heard that some men want to kill you," José said. "They wanted me to join them, but I said no. I fear the judgment of God." His black eyes darted back and forth. "What is that book, anyway?"

"It's a wonderful book," the other man answered, holding up the small volume. "It tells about God's judgment, because He is holy, but it also tells about His mercy, because He is love."

"I know about God's judgment," José answered soberly. "I think about it all the time—I fear it. But I don't know anything about God's mercy and love."

"Here, would you like to borrow it? It's called the Good News of Mark."

José took the book eagerly and walked away. "However, it's too late for me to receive God's mercy," he murmured to himself. "I'm completely lost in this darkness."

Those shadows of darkness, though, didn't stop José's trembling fingers from opening the little book, the Good News of Mark. He began to read and read for hours into the night. He read the whole thing, his mind and heart full of questions. Somehow the words seemed to shine a glimmer of light into his soul.

"This is about Jesus," he murmured. "Yet this Jesus is so different from the one I've always heard about. I only knew judgment and demands. I never knew He showed such love."

So many questions. So much José didn't understand. Finally he cried out, "This love is not for me! I'm still under the judgment of God!"

José drank more and more liquor, but could find no peace. The darkness of the spirit world seemed to close in on him.

One day, a group of men came to the coffee plantation where José worked, right into the home of the plantation owner, with Bibles. *Didn't they know their lives were in danger? They could be killed on any road, these evangélicos!* José listened as the leader, Pastor Vicente, read from the Good News of John, the story of a man named Nicodemus who came to Jesus and learned that he needed to be born again.

"This 'born again' is the beginning of a whole new life!" Vicente explained. "Look, here is my friend, Brother Marco Franco. He used to drink himself drunk every weekend. He used to swing his machete at anyone who argued with him. But Jesus Christ has come and made him a new man. He's full of love for others. He has been born again."

José listened, all the muscles in his face tense and his teeth clenched. He was drawn to these words. Why did he also feel like he wanted to push them away? Was it those dark forces at work in his life?

Even though he wanted to talk with the evangélicos so much, for some reason he refused to speak to them or even shake their hands. But he watched them walk away with terror. Had they spoken truth? Was there hope? How in the world did someone get this new birth?

In a box of old moldy books, José found a set of all four Gospels. He began to read and read and read. "I see that this gospel means power," he said, "I know it's a good kind of power, not evil power like that priest or like that s-s-spirit." He trembled as he said the word. "However, I don't understand how to get it."

As he picked the coffee beans on the plantation, he could look out over the surrounding hills. All around, in this mountainous area of Colombia, the mountain trails were visible for miles and miles. Many days José could see the small group of evangélicos plod along the narrow paths, trekking from one village to another with their small bag of New Testaments. *Why do they do that? That new birth, it has to be worth a lot, because they give up everything for it. Why do they risk their lives this way?* There had to be some sort of power here, some sort of riches here, that José didn't understand at all.

When he was finally able to get a complete New Testament, José marveled at the stories in the book of Acts. "These men have power like I've never dreamed of! These are the same men as in those Gospels, but now they're fearless!"

He began to read the letters of Paul. "The God of the universe has placed everything under the power of Christ," he read, "and has set Him up as head of everything for the church. For the church is His body, and in that body lives fully the One who fills the whole wide universe."

José could hardly believe what he read. "This is power! This is riches! How can I have it?"

One day, he decided. "I'll become an evangélico. I won't smoke or drink any more. I won't go to the drinking parties any more. And I'll spend all my time reading the New Testament."

However, José still wasn't free from his prison. He still felt the darkness and the fear of the holy God's judgment. He struggled with cravings to smoke and drink. His face never even smiled, and he couldn't be friendly with his fellow workers.

"Hey, José!" The other plantation workers laughed. "You may be strange, but you're no evangélico!" Where was the joy Paul talked about in his New Testament letters? Where was the power? Then a thought came to him. *You still have that box of books. It's still stored under your bed. That power book is still buried at the bottom of that box.*

"That's it!" thought José. "The demonic power came when I concentrated really hard and said some special words. I had to open myself to the spirit powers. Maybe, that's the way to do it with God. If I concentrate really hard, and open myself to the power of God's Spirit instead of Satan, and say some special words, then I might get the power, life and joy of the evangélicos. That's got to be what they did. Maybe, if I get out that book and study the incantations and charms, only this time I think about God … ."

Even before he could finish his thought, José's body convulsed with shakes. He thought he was going to be sick. He felt a sense of terror at the thought of even touching that book again. There was no way he could say those words.

No, that couldn't be it. "I'll find the answer in the New Testament," he determined. "And I'll ask God. And … and I'll ask one of those evangélicos. This time, I really will tell him that I want to know Jesus Christ and understand and believe."

However, the next time José had an opportunity to go to an evangélico meeting, the evil power came over him again. Before he could even ask the question, that was such a desperate cry in his soul, he ran to another room. He went face down all the way to the floor and writhed in agony.

"God! God!" he cried out. "I said I would come to Jesus Christ today, but I can't! Show me how to be released from this terror! Break these chains!"

He sat up, and something felt different. "I will go forward," he murmured. "I will not go back."

He walked back into the room where the evangélicos were meeting. They were singing *"Oh, I want to walk with Christ."*

José began to sing. *"Oh, I want to walk with Christ!"* It was the cry of his soul.

And suddenly, quietly, the holy God of heaven, the Father of mercy and love, did the mighty work. He touched José and rescued him.

José was free. The chains were broken.

The heavy burden lifted.

The dark presence disappeared.

José had found real riches, the kind that couldn't be stolen away. He had found real power, the kind that couldn't be destroyed.

José was a new man, born again into Jesus Christ.

* * *

José Pinzon began to travel the hills with the other evangélicos, where his life was often in danger. Men, who determined they would kill the Christian preachers, often threatened him and tried to attack him. For many years, he continued to travel and preach, telling everyone how they could find the true riches, the heavenly riches, in Jesus Christ alone. He told them how they could receive great honor by becoming sons of the holy God, the Father of mercy and love. He told them how they could know the greatest power in the world by finding freedom from the dark forces of Satan through the power of the mighty Savior, Jesus Christ.

The transformation, the power, of his own life was living proof.

See Thinking Further for Chapter 4 on page 137.

5. VICTOR AND THE DREAM HUT

A voice called, "Victor, Victor! The people in that hut are dying without Christ! No one has ever told them!"

Victor Landero sat up in bed. What kind of strange dream was that? He closed his eyes and saw the hut again, as clearly as if he stood there. He saw the thatched roof, the simple wooden fence, the gate. There it was.

But that strange voice …

He lay back down in bed and tried to sleep. "I'm working for you, Lord. I tell many people about You," he murmured as he drifted off.

There was the hut again. "Victor, Victor!" the voice called. "The people in that hut are dying without Christ! No one has ever told them!"

This time when Victor sat up, he felt a cold sweat all over his body. Why did he have that dream again? And anyway, how in the world could he find such a hut?

The gospel was spreading in the lowlands of Colombia in the 1960s. Any time someone came in to buy anything in Victor's small store, he spoke to them about Jesus. Then there were enough believers to make an entire congregation, to gather together for worship every week. Victor and his family moved to another area and began to tell other people who had never heard. Persecution against the evangélicos had died down, and people were willing to listen to this amazing story of the True and Living Way.

No one preached the gospel more diligently than Victor Landero. The good news of the great salvation through Jesus Christ went out with vigor in his area, and one new Christian after another could say, "We learned of the evangelio through Victor Landero!" Or maybe they heard from someone who heard from someone who heard from Victor Landero.

But this dream … what was he to do?

For days and then weeks and then months, Victor tried to push the dream out of his mind. Yet still he heard that voice, "The people in that hut are dying without Christ! No one has ever told them!"

Finally, one day, Victor said to his wife, "I have to go find that hut in my dream."

"But your daughter is sick, Victor," his wife said. "What if she dies?"

Victor thought long and hard about that one. "If she dies," he said, "she'll be in the arms of Jesus, because she has trusted in Him. But there's someone out there, in a hut with a thatched roof, who has never heard about Jesus. Can you trust Jesus for her protection with me?" Slowly, his wife nodded.

Victor knelt beside the bed of his little girl, and prayed with her. The next morning, he prayed with her again, kissed her goodbye, hugged and kissed his wife, and started off.

"O my loving Shepherd," Victor prayed. "I have no idea where I'm going. Will You lead me as You did Abraham?" He began to walk.

He walked and walked. And he prayed, "Heavenly Father, my faithful Guide, I trust You to take me to that hut in my dream. I remember what it looks like. I remember the fence, the gate and the thatched roof. I trust You to take me there."

For a whole day, Victor walked. "Am I going the right way, Lord?" he murmured. He settled down to sleep for the night.

The next day, he began to walk again. "I trust You to lead me," he whispered as he made his way through the dark woods.

And then … there it was.

A small hut in the clearing at the edge of the woods. The thatched roof, the simple wooden fence, the gate. All of it was there, exactly like in his dream.

"You've brought me here," Victor murmured. "Surely, You have prepared the way." He walked up to the hut and knocked on the door.

A woman opened it. "Yes?" She knit her brow in surprise to see a strange man before her.

"My name is Victor Landero. I would like your permission to invite your neighbors to a meeting here tonight. I want to tell everyone around here about the evangelio of Jesus Christ, the gospel." What would she think?

The woman's eyes opened wide, and she began to tremble. Did she feel fear? Shock? Horror?

"I don't mean to trouble you," Victor faltered, "but in a dream, I saw a hut exactly like this one. God told me I had to bring the evangelio to the people here. Then He led me to you."

The woman nodded slowly, without a word, as if she were in a trance. She slowly opened the door wide to let Victor come in and sit in the only chair.

After resting for a bit, Victor spent the afternoon knocking on the doors in the surrounding area, inviting people to come hear about the evangelio. That night, twenty-four people gathered in the woman's tiny hut to listen to Victor's words, all of them wide-eyed and wanting to hear this good news from God.

Quietly, carefully, Victor explained the true gospel of Jesus Christ from the New Testament, the gospel of the love of the heavenly Father for vile unworthy sinners, His great salvation of sinners from hell, through faith in Christ alone. "Would anyone here like to put all faith and trust in Jesus Christ alone?" Victor finally asked.

Every hand went up.

Surely they don't understand, Victor thought. He began again to tell the whole story, emphasizing the new life in Christ, the life that no longer lives for self but lives for God and others.

"Now, how many of you would like to put all your faith and trust in Jesus Christ alone, and have a transformed life?" he finally asked again.

Every hand went up. Several voices broke the silence. "We understood you the first time," they said.

So Victor led them all in prayer to trust in Jesus Christ. "I'd like to meet with you here again tomorrow night," he added.

After the people had gone back to their homes, the woman spoke to Victor again, her voice trembling. "You said that you had a dream. Three nights ago … I had a dream as well. I dreamed that my house was full of people. Full, so full there was no room for any more." She waved her arm as Victor looked around the now-

empty one-room hut. She went on. "I dreamed that a strange man, a man I'd never seen before, stood there with a book. He used this word again and again: *evangelio*. It was a word I'd never heard before. He taught us to sing songs about this evangelio." She gazed at him with fear and wonder in her eyes. "And now, you're here."

"Then the true God prepared you too." Victor thought soberly about the timing of her dream. It was the night before he determined that he would go. "Even before I told you about this evangelio, you already knew that was from God."

The next night, all the people returned, bringing ten more with them. All ten of them also trusted in Christ.

Victor stayed three more days. He gave them a Bible to share, taught them gospel songs, prayed with them, and then returned to his home. He found that while he was gone, the gracious Healer had given health to his little girl. "Thank You, our loving Father," he prayed with his family. "We knew she was safe in Your arms, whether she lived or died. We thank You that You have kept her here with us."

* * *

A year later, a missionary from the United States, David Howard, visited the group of Christians around the hut in the clearing. He found that all of the original believers were still there, and they had brought even more people to Christ, to make a congregation of about fifty fervent Christians. Every night, they met to listen to someone read the Bible, discuss it, and to sing and pray together. Their lives had been truly transformed.

Victor taught many Christians to become evangelists in their own areas. As more and more went out, many believers were scattered throughout the countryside area, like bright candles in the darkness of Colombia.

When there were thousands of believers there, Victor left that area and began to work among the Embera Indians of Colombia, where there were no Christians. The work there was very difficult, with few converts. When David Howard later asked him about that very slow work, compared to the hundreds and thousands of Colombians he had seen come to Christ, Victor answered, "I know other people have labored long with little result, but it doesn't matter. I'll stay here among these Indians for the rest of my life, because this is where God has called me."

See Thinking Further for Chapter 5 on page 137.

6. RUSSELL AND THE PICTURE BOOK

Four-year-old Russell Stendal snuggled on his father's lap. It was story time.

"This is a new book, Russ," said Dad. "We'll learn a little about people in other countries, and we'll pray for them, that they'll know Jesus."

Russell was very curious to know about people in other countries. All he knew about was his happy life in Minnesota, where his dad went to work at a job someplace every day and his mother took care of him in their cozy home on a tree-lined street, where Mom and Dad told him Bible stories and sang songs about Jesus with him every night at bedtime. He went to Sunday school and church every week. This was life in the United States in 1959.

Dad showed Russell a book about a native tribe in South America who lived in the Andes Mountains. The black and white photos showed huge peaks. "Look at that sky, Russell. Just think how tall those mountains are." It was hard to imagine. "See, they took these pictures from an airplane, so you could see all those huts down in that valley."

There was a close-up photo of the tribal people, dressed in simple cloth, working on their small farm with simple tools. Another photo showed them as they took the produce of their little farms to sell at the streetside market. They hoped to earn some money and buy the important supplies they needed.

Then Dad turned the page. Russell was horrified. "What's happening in those pictures, Dad?" There, the men were spending their few cents on liquor.

In that one, they were getting drunk.

In the next one, they started to fight, with machetes, attacking each other and wounding each other. Women and children gazed into the open door of the dark saloon, wide-eyed and fearful.

"What's happening?"

"Uh, Russ, uh, I didn't know," Dad stammered.

The last picture of that set showed a tribal woman with her children hunched beside the mountain trail. Before them lay the man of the family, who had passed out from drunkenness. When he awoke, they would trudge back up the mountain trail with no oil or salt or other necessities. All the money was gone, spent on liquor.

The next week, this dreary cycle would start all over again.

Dad closed the book and repeated, "Russ, I didn't know ... It wasn't the way I thought ... ."

But Russell barely heard him. "Why do they live like that?" he demanded.

"Well, I guess it's because they don't know any better."

That answer wasn't good enough. "Why don't they know any better?"

Dad hesitated. "I guess it's because no one has ever shown them a better way."

Russell felt the tears of indignation sting his eyes. "Why hasn't anyone shown them a better way?"

Dad hesitated again, stumbling over his words. He knew he didn't have a good answer. "I guess because no one has ever cared to go."

Russell answered loudly and almost angrily. "But *you* care, don't you, Dad? *You* care! *You* can tell them! Why don't *we* go?"

Dad looked around at the comfortable living room with its sleek couch and its corner table with the large family Bible. He thought about the thirty-million-dollar dam construction project he had just finished and the big promotion he had just been offered.

He sighed and ran his fingers through his hair. "It's not that easy, Russ. We can't just jump on a plane and go to South America. Why that's ... becoming a

missionary, and if people become missionaries, well …
God has to call them. They have to be sure God wants
them to go there. God would have to show them the
way. He'd have to provide the money …" Dad's voice
trailed off.

Then he sat up and patted his son and smiled. "Tell
you what, Russ. When you grow up, maybe God will
call you to be a missionary and you can go to these
Indians in South America."

Russell had already begun to slide off his dad's lap.
He knelt down right there at the couch and began to
pray very loudly. "Dear heavenly Father, please call my
parents to be missionaries right now! I don't want to
have to wait until I grow up to tell those Indians about
Jesus!"

* * *

Four years later, the Stendal family landed in
Bogotá, the capital city of Colombia. Russell's dad had
quit his high-paying job. His parents had sold their
house, gone to language school, and joined Wycliffe
Bible Translators. They were ready to find a primitive
tribal people in the mountains who had never heard of
Jesus Christ.

God led the Stendals to two small tribal men who
stood only four and a half feet tall, about the same
height as Russell, who was now eight years old. These

small men came from a native tribe called the Kogis, who lived high, high up in the Sierra Nevada Mountains of northern Colombia. From them, the Stendals planned to study their language and prepare to move far up the mountain to take the gospel to the entire tribe.

One day, a pilot who helped with Wycliffe Bible Translators saw Chad Stendal, Russell's dad, with the Kogi men. He saw that these two small men looked completely different from the other people of Colombia. He saw their long, matted, black hair, their short stature, and their dirty-white cotton smocks.

"Hey!" the pilot called. "Where did you get those little Indians?"

Chad wasn't too surprised at the question. After all, those "little Indians" had already attracted a lot of attention everywhere he took them.

"Oh, up in the northern part of the country," he answered casually.

"What do you mean, the northern part of the country?" The man seemed agitated. "Where, exactly?"

"In the mountains. What's wrong?"

The pilot still wasn't satisfied with that answer. "You've got to show me on a map. Are these two the only ones, or are there more?"

Chad wanted to laugh at such a question. "Of course there are more. There are thousands of them up there."

"I can't believe this; this is impossible. This can't be." The pilot muttered under his breath as he hurried inside to find a large map and spread it on the floor. "Point to it," he insisted.

Chad pointed to the high mountains in northern Colombia, the Sierra Nevadas near Santa Marta.

"I can't believe it," the other man muttered again. "Impossible. These things just don't happen."

"What in the world are you talking about?" By now other people had gathered around, including Cameron Townsend, the founder of Wycliffe Bible Translators.

The pilot ran his fingers through his hair and looked around. "I'm almost embarrassed to tell you," he said, "but I have this brother-in-law who had some sort of prophecy or vision or something." He cleared his throat and continued. "He said that God had shown him that the Word of God would go to a little people who lived high in the mountains in the northeast of Colombia, little people with strange customs. When he found out I was on my way to Colombia, he asked me to find those little people and tell him who they were. I said, 'There aren't any pygmies in Colombia, only in Africa!' But he didn't believe me, and I tell you, he and his wife have prayed for those little Indians ever since God spoke to them, even though they didn't know anything else about them. I can't even believe I'm telling you this."

He rested his chin on his hands and gazed in wonder at the two small Kogi men, who watched him, silently. Chad Stendal and the others turned to gaze as well.

Cameron Townsend looked sober. "More people like this should have a burden to pray for our Bibleless tribes," he said.

The pilot got a camera and took a picture of the two Kogi men standing with his own son. Then he stuck the

picture in an envelope to mail back to Washington to his sister and brother-in-law. "Thought you might like to know," was all he wrote.

Art and Verdie Sather were the man and woman who had prayed for the Kogi tribe without even knowing their names. They were overjoyed to see the photograph that confirmed what they already knew. Immediately they wrote to Wycliffe, eager to obtain more information and to make contact with the Stendal family.

Without fail, they prayed for Chad and Pat Stendal and their family. Without fail, they prayed for the Kogi tribe. They had already been praying for them, faithfully. Now they had a photo and they knew the names.

See Thinking Further for Chapter 6 on page 138.

7. "I MAKE THE SUN RISE"

ow could the Stendal family convince the Kogi tribes that they had come to help them, not hurt them? Their two Kogi friends, Santiago and Alfonso, had welcomed them, but that village had only four families. All the other Kogis hated and feared outsiders. They remembered the terrible stories that had been handed down by storytellers for over eight hundred years of the Spanish conquerors who had treated their ancestors so cruelly, that the Kogis had hidden away, far and high up in the mountains. They swore they would never again let outsiders come in.

Therefore, they were determined that these outsiders wouldn't be any different.

The Stendal family continued to live in their own hut, among the four Kogi families. They learned their language, treated their illnesses, taught them cleaner living habits, and told them about the true God and His Son, Jesus Christ. Someone from Gospel Recordings came and helped them record Bible stories in the Kogi language. Russell and his younger brother and sisters learned to hunt, trap, fish, and make tools like the ones the Kogis used. They collected unusual animals for pets, like parrots, alligators, toucans, marmosets, and different kinds of snakes. Sometimes, they kept the pets with them as they did their math and reading in the corner of the hut, or outside under a tree. They were having a great time in Colombia.

However, Chad Stendal wondered. "Surely, Lord, You don't want me to stop with four Kogi families, do You? O Heavenly Father, I cry out to You to make a way for me to go to more villages!"

One day, the news came. "Chief Nacio is dying," Santiago reported with agitation. "He wants you to come."

"What? Really?" Chad was stunned. Chief Nacio was the head of all of Mamarongo, the largest Kogi village on the entire western side of the mountain. Chad knew by now that a Kogi chief was vitally important to his people. If he died before a young man had been trained to take his place, the whole village, possibly even the whole tribe, would fear that the entire world would sink into darkness. They thought the world might even end if this chief died.

"He called for all the different witchdoctors," Santiago continued. "None of them can heal him. He has prayed to the ancient mother, but she hasn't heard him. Now he's almost dead. I went to him and saw him so weak he could barely even sit up. I told him that everyone you help around here has recovered."

It was true. Every single person that Chad had treated had gotten well. It was miraculous, they knew.

"Chief Nacio controls all the weather," Santiago went on. "He controls the sun, the wind, the wet season and the dry season. He knows how to say the words to bring the sun up in the morning, and do the dance for nine days so my people can get ready to plant. Yet he hasn't finished training anyone to take his place, and my people don't know what to do."

Chad sighed. It was hard to listen to this. He had heard stories about the way the chiefs were trained. Young boys were taken from their mothers and kept in the dark much of the time, for the first eighteen years of their lives, while they memorized hundreds of ancient stories and secret rituals. If any of them lived long enough to make it through all the training, they were eligible to become chiefs.

Nothing was written down, so everything had to be passed on by the chief. The chief taught them which offering to make to which spirits and what words to say when people became sick, when they had conflicts with an enemy, or broke one of the hundreds of rules of the spirit world. This religion was a prison of darkness.

This time, it was Chief Nacio himself who was on his deathbed, and all the chiefs and witchdoctors from the surrounding villages had come. They expected their rituals to work, but no one knew the right magic words to say to give any help to the dying chief.

"He doesn't really want you to come," said Santiago bluntly. "He's tried everything else."

"You said he was at the point of death, right, Santiago?"

"Yes."

"What will happen if I come to help him, but he still dies?"

Santiago thought for a moment. "The people of his village will kill you. Nevertheless, he won't die if you come, because everyone you help gets well."

Chad felt his face break out into a sweat. He looked around, at the little hut Santiago had built for him to live in. He looked at his wife, Patty, patiently tending to their little baby, at Russell and his younger brother as they played and shouted together. *Is it right, Lord? Is it right for me to go?*

Santiago added, "The trip will take three days, you know."

Chad nodded slowly, deep in thought. He knew. Three days of rough travel over huge, rushing rivers with no bridges. Down steep cliffs and up steep mountains. On narrow trails alongside the mountain where they would have to walk single file. If they stepped off to one side, they could tumble for hundreds of feet.

"Santiago, I have to ask the Lord if it's right for me to go to Chief Nacio."

Santiago nodded. He knew enough about this strange, tall, pale man with powerful medicine to know that he often had to talk to that Lord.

Chad went inside and looked around his tiny hut, which was so different from that comfortable house on a quiet, tree-lined street in Minnesota with its cushioned couch and modern kitchen. Here they had a bed, a handmade bench, a handmade table. In the corner was the big pot of water that someone had to fetch every day by climbing all the way down the steep, long bank of the river and back up.

"Lord, should I stay here, in Santiago's village, with four families?" Chad prayed. "Or should I go to Chief Nacio's village and risk my life to bring them the good news of the Savior? If You want me to go, I'll go, and if you want me to stay, I'll stay."

For a moment Chad was silent, but only a moment. It seemed that the voice of the Lord rang out loud and clear. "Go!"

Chad jumped. He felt as if he had been struck by a powerful wind. "All right, Lord! I'll go!"

Quickly, he went outside and told Santiago. Santiago's face broke out into a huge grin. Together, they began to pack the big bags. They loaded them on the backs of the bueys; big, strong, pack animals like oxen that were so sure-footed, they could easily traverse the high, treacherous mountains.

Chad said goodbye to his family, and they started off.

For three days they climbed up and down mountains, crossed rushing rivers, and trudged along the paths. They stopped at the homes of people Santiago knew. The Kogis almost jumped in fear at the sight of this tall, blond man with strange clothing, and some of them cried out in fright. But because of Santiago, they gave him food. "Don't eat the food in Mamarango," they warned. "Chief Nacio's people will try to poison you."

Chad realized he was the first non-Kogi man to travel these trails for hundreds of years ... or maybe ... ever. He began to see more and more Kogi houses in the distance among the mountains, and Kogi people along the trail. All of them were frightened to see him.

Finally, Chad and Santiago reached Mamarango: the village of Chief Nacio.

"That's the chief's wife," Santiago murmured.

"He's dying!" the woman cried out. "He eats no more."

Chad's heart began to beat harder. *What if he dies after I see him?* "I have to trust You, Lord," he prayed. "You told

66

me to come." He bent his tall frame to enter the low, small doorway of the chief's dark, dark hut. The smoke filled his eyes, but finally, in the darkness, he could see a small figure in a hammock. It was the dying chief.

Chad watched as Chief Nacio took hold of the edge of the hammock, and with great effort brought himself to a sitting position. He looked like a skeleton, with thin skin stretched across small bones, and ankles that were badly swollen. When he spoke, Chad had to lean forward to catch his words.

"I bring up ... the sun ... in the morning." Chief Nacio weakly swept his arm across the dark, windowless room.

He coughed and breathed heavily. "By my sacred dance ... I bring the time of no rain."

His eyes, bright with fever in his hollow face, gazed ahead. "I control ... all things ... in these mountains. All things ... in this valley ... are in the palm of my hand."

Then he looked straight at Chad. His breath came in a heavy wheeze, and his ghostly voice spoke again. "I have you ... in the palm of my hand ... as well." With the little strength he had, he jabbed one finger into his other palm and snapped his hand closed over it.

Then he lay back down in the hammock and touched his red and swollen neck. He turned his face to the side. "This is not ... the time ... for me to die! I am ... not old! My hair ... is not white! I haven't yet ... trained

my apprentices! All the wisdom … that is passed on … from chief to chief … will be … lost!"

Chad looked at the emaciated body. He knew that no medicine could save Chief Nacio. He looked at the chief's hip, where he would usually give a shot. There was no hip. It was only skin stretched over bone.

"Chief," he said boldly, "It's too late for medicine to save you, but the true God, whom I serve, can still heal you. If you are healed, you need to promise to give the praise to Him."

"Yes," answered the chief weakly. What choice did he have? He raised his hand from his hammock, but it dropped back down. Chad administered some medicine through a shot into the hip, but because there was no place for it to go, it just flowed right back out. He prayed over Chief Nacio for healing from the heavenly Healer, and then he left that dark, oppressive hut.

The chief lay in his hammock, fighting for every breath.

Chad walked on with a heavy heart. He and Santiago trekked to the hut where they would stay, down the steep river bank, across the river, and up the steep bank on the other side.

There, some Kogis brought them food. Chad looked at it and remembered the warning. "Don't eat the food in Mamarango. It will be poisoned."

Lord, what should I do? They probably want to poison me, but if it's not poisoned, then to refuse it would be terribly rude.

After a brief inward struggle, Chad decided to leave his life in his Father's hands once again. He ate everything they gave him and went to sleep, trusting God for the results.

Early the next morning, as Chad and Santiago ate their breakfast, they saw three men approaching from the other side of the river. As the three men climbed down the steep bank, crossed the river, and climbed up the other side, Chad gasped. *That's Chief Nacio!*

He was the man in the middle. His ankles were no longer swollen. His neck was no longer swollen. The expression on his face radiated peace and joy. Chad felt his forehead and could tell that the fever was gone. *He was healed.*

"Your God has restored my life," the chief said simply.

Just like in the New Testament. "Chief, you promised to give Him thanks and praise."

"Yes." Chief Nacio kneeled on the ground right there and prayed his first prayer to the true God. "Living God, I know You are the living God. You have restored my life. I praise You."

"Hey," whispered Santiago to Chad. "This is a good time to listen to those Bible stories on that thing." He pointed to the audio player with the Gospel Recordings Bible stories on it.

"Now?" asked Chad. There stood Chief Nacio with his two assistants. Now? Chief Nacio was the grand storyteller of the Kogis—he knew hundreds of ancient stories from the Kogi legends. What if he didn't like those Bible stories? After all, he and Santiago were still eating his food.

"Yes, now," said Santiago. "It's my own voice they'll hear, so they'll know the stories are good."

Chad turned on the audio player. What would Chief Nacio think of these stories? Especially the ones that talked about the death and resurrection of Jesus Christ?

Santiago's voice began to come out of the strange little black box. Other Kogis began to gather timidly, watchfully. Chief Nacio listened with his head cocked to one side, wondering about this strange contraption.

Then he began to nod. He nodded and nodded. By the time the audio player had finished, the chief said, "These are real stories. Send out an order!" he commanded in a loud voice. "I want all Kogis from all around to come listen to these stories! Even the blind and the lame must come!"

The next day, dozens of Kogis assembled. They were all short, none taller than five feet. Many of them looked very sickly, their faces yellow; their long black hair tangled, matted, and dirty; their clothes stained and rotting.

They had never before seen a man so tall and so pale as Chad Stendal.

Chad played the recordings for them all. Santiago beamed as he listened again to his own voice that told the real stories.

When the stories had finished, Chad offered medicine to anyone who wanted it.

"You can come back!" Chief Nacio proclaimed. "You can come visit in Mamarango any time. We will always welcome you."

* * *

Chad and his family all eventually moved to Mamarango, and were even able to install an airstrip in the mountains where a small plane could land. This was against great opposition, because even though the chief had approved, many Kogis from different areas around the mountain still believed that if they had contact with the outside world, the world would come to an end.

The Lord didn't immediately bring a great work of the Spirit to the Kogi people. Work among them progressed slowly, but the few people who came to Christ stood firm. In the face of great persecution and threats of death, they have stood strong for Jesus Christ and continue to reach out to their own people.

See Thinking Further for Chapter 7 on page 138.

8. MACHINE GUNS AND A TYPEWRITER

The kidnaper, a young man with a black mustache, dressed in camouflage and holding a machine gun, strode over to Russell with a sneer on his face. He kicked him. "You Americans! You're all spies who want to destroy Colombia! And now you shot one of our men! You're a worthless dog!" The kidnaper pointed to another man who sat on a log, grimacing, while a woman bandaged his leg.

Russell Stendal, twenty-eight years old, lay on the ground and looked up. "I'm not a spy," he protested. "I'm a missionary. I shot him just because I wanted to escape—you would have done the same thing, wouldn't you?"

The man snorted and turned away.

"Listen," Russell continued, "I've been in Colombia all my life, since I was eight years old. My parents are missionaries to the Kogi Indians. I love the Colombian people—I want to help them."

Communist revolutionaries, which some people called guerrillas, had taken over parts of Colombia, wanting to overthrow the government. Most of them hated the terrible division between rich and poor, as the poor struggled for existence. Like Robin Hood, they planned to steal from the rich in order to help the poor. But all too often, they ended up just stealing from the poor, mainly because it was so much easier. They spent the money on more weapons for more terrorism to try to take over the government.

But now, here was a rich American! He would bring a fine ransom. Millions of dollars, maybe! Those Americans were so rich!

The revolutionaries took Russell to their secret camp hidden deep in the jungle, where no plane that flew overhead would ever see them. Here they tied him to a tree like a dog. Then they wrote a letter to demand a ransom payment for him.

"Don't think I have a lot of money," Russell told them. "I don't. I'm just a Christian missionary."

"I don't believe all that Christian garbage about love and mercy." Nancy, the nurse for the revolutionaries, spat on the ground. "You don't believe it either. If you did, you wouldn't have shot our comrade when we captured you. You hated him." She waved her hand in his face and walked over to the camp kitchen, a little spot between the trees with a small fire and some tin pots.

"I didn't hate him," Russell answered. "I didn't really want to hurt him; I just wanted to get away.

Nevertheless, I told you I didn't have a gun, and that was wrong. I shouldn't have lied. Rather, I should have trusted God to protect me. It was wrong to lie."

It was wrong to lie? The revolutionaries lied all the time. Their lives were built on lies. They knew their leaders lied to them. They lied to each other. They lied to their captives. Of course they expected him to lie. Yet, he said it was wrong to lie?

He admitted that he did something wrong? The revolutionaries *never* admitted they had done anything wrong!

Grudgingly, Nancy brought him some beans on a tin plate and some black coffee. She could see already that this man was different from the others they had captured.

Russell looked around at the camp. Almost all of his kidnapers were younger than he was, and some of them even looked like teenagers. And here he was, seated on a rough wooden bench with a rope around his neck, tied to a tree. If he wasn't careful, they might just get impatient and shoot him.

Russell put his chin in his hands and thought about his wife and little girl. "Father in heaven, aren't You going to help me get out of here?" he prayed. "Should I try to get away?" He began to try to figure out a way to escape, but if he tried and didn't make it … he would be a dead man.

Days passed while Russell sat. He sweated from the heat, swatted mosquitoes, watched the men clean their weapons, and listened to the lectures. Those revolutionaries took hours and hours every day to listen to the philosophy of communism.

Sometimes, Russell tried to talk a little with whichever one of the men was assigned to guard him, walking back and forth with the machine gun pointed at him. Every night, with the rope still around him, he climbed into a hammock under a mosquito net. All night long the guards shone flashlights on his face to make sure he hadn't escaped.

"I've got to get away!" Russell thought again and again. "I need to be rescued!"

"What about your kidnapers?" God said. *"Don't they need to be rescued? They've been taken prisoner in a different way. They don't know how to escape."*

Russell remembered that when he used to fly his plane to sell fish for the Colombian fishermen, sometimes he flew over areas where he knew the communist revolutionaries hid. He had prayed for them, that they would hear the gospel too.

Maybe this was the time.

"I'd like to write," Russell announced one morning. "Can you give me pencil and paper?" After all, day after day he just sat there with nothing to do.

"If you want to write a letter, you can write only what we tell you," one of them said.

"No," said Russell. "I'm going to write a book."

"Ha, ha!" said the boss. "Sure, let him write a book."

With a rope around his neck, Russell began to write. He wrote about life in the revolutionary camp, and each of the revolutionaries he spoke with. He wrote about his childhood among the Kogi Indians. He wrote about how he had learned to fly a plane when he was nineteen. He wrote about the fishing business he developed to help the poor Colombians earn a living. He wrote about the forgiveness of a loving God, the justice and power of a holy God.

He also wrote about mistakes he had made. Bad things he had done.

I don't have to be without sin, Father. I just have to be honest, before You and before man. This is what it means to be poor in spirit.

Before long, the revolutionaries gathered around him more and more, because they wanted to read each page as he wrote it. Then, somehow, one of them found him a typewriter, and they let him type for several hours each day. Whenever they could, the revolutionaries clustered around him and read every page as it came out of the typewriter. Sometimes they laughed. Sometimes they went away deep in thought. Sometimes they argued.

"How can a man who's educated like you possibly believe in God?" Giovanni, one of the leaders, waved Russell's paper in his face. "The only reason religion was invented was so the rich people could keep poor people enslaved. But now, with education, communism will soon liberate all the countries, and then we'll solve all the world's problems. We'll make sure everyone in the world has enough to eat, and we'll eliminate disease and poverty."

"You try to bring world peace through terrible crimes and terrorism," Russell challenged him. "How can you do that? You kidnaped me; you might even kill me, when I haven't done anything wrong. How can you sow injustice and expect to reap justice? How can you sow bad things and expect to reap good things?"

That night, as Russell lay in his hammock under the mosquito net, he woke up with each flash of the flashlight. With every flash, all night long, he prayed, "O Father in heaven! Would you rescue these captors?"

See Thinking Further for Chapter 8 on page 139.

9. RESCUE THE KIDNAPERS

Weeks passed while Russell waited for release. He knew that his family was doing all they could to find a way to get him free, to make a deal with his kidnapers. On one occasion, his family sent him a Bible, some other books, and a package of candy. Russell decided to play a trick on the revolutionaries.

"Candy from the U.S. is better than any candy you could ever get around here," he boasted as he munched a purple one. "Do you want to try it?" He took a red one and broke it up into smaller parts as Nancy and several of the young men gathered around.

For a moment, he watched them eat. Then he jumped up. "I did it!" he cried. "The red candy was poisoned, and you'll all die in five minutes!"

The revolutionaries looked terrified. Their faces turned white. But five minutes passed and nothing happened.

Russell began to laugh. He laughed and laughed, pointing at them. "I was just joking!" he said. "You looked white as a sheet! Now you know what it feels like, don't you?"

Some of them chuckled nervously. Some of them were angry. However, when that story came out of Russell's typewriter, the other men laughed till their sides ached. "He got you! He got you good!"

It was clear, nevertheless, that the kidnapers were afraid to die. One day, one of the young men asked him, "What will you do if your family can't pay our price?"

"Well, I know they can't afford very much," Russell replied. "So you could just take whatever they give you, or … you could kill me."

"Aren't you afraid to die?"

Russell shook his head. "I know it would be uncomfortable," he said. "But no, I'm not afraid."

The young man turned away soberly. *How could anyone be unafraid to die? What kind of strength was this?*

When that young man had a chance, he whispered, "I wish I could be a Christian like you. I think you're right about God, and there's no way that the teachings of Jesus can work with the teachings of communism. But I can't leave the revolutionaries."

"Why not?" Russell asked.

"I took an oath when I joined, and if I leave, they can kill me. I wish I had met you before I became a revolutionary."

More and more, the kidnapers began to enjoy Russell's company. During the day, they began to let him walk loose in the camp. They eagerly waited for each page of his book as it came out of the typewriter. They discussed the ideas he wrote about with each other. Sometimes, they played chess with him, and almost all of them loved to talk and argue with him. They argued about evolution, about communism, about the existence of God, about weakness and strength. They went away amazed at the wisdom of his answers.

Every day, Russell read and meditated on a Psalm. He read the Bible out loud, even when the men grumbled about it and acted like they didn't want to hear.

More and more, the younger revolutionaries questioned the orders that they used to follow without thinking.

"Why do we have to kill so many innocent people?" they asked. "Why do we want to take over the drug business when it's so bad—why don't we destroy it instead? Why do we fight evil with evil? How can that bring true peace? If there really is a God, then we're in big trouble!"

As the weeks turned into months, Russell prayed for his kidnapers more and more, until every night in his hammock, he prayed for hours, for all of them to find true freedom in Jesus Christ, to be released from their captivity. Even though some of the revolutionaries did and said things to try to make him afraid, he still felt great peace.

One day, Russell talked with Giovanni for two hours. Afterwards, the leader broke down and said, "I want to get right with God, but my case is hopeless. I've done too many terrible, awful, vile things.

"It's never too late," Russell encouraged him. "There's no sin too great. The bigger the mess, the more grateful we'll be when God gives us freedom." From that point on, Giovanni no longer argued with him.

But one man, Mariano, still despised him. "Why did Jesus have to die?" he demanded one day. "If He came from God, it would have been good enough just to give us a message about mercy and love. However, you say that He died on purpose. That's a story for weaklings and fools. If I were God and came down to earth, I wouldn't let anyone nail me to a cross! I would have called down all the angels and defended myself. An all-powerful God would never have let Himself be put to death. This shows that you just made up this story!"

Russell paused and prayed. Finally, he said, "Jesus died because we've all been kidnaped." He looked around at the revolutionaries in the camp with their hopeless faces and continued. "We've been kidnaped by our own selfishness and pride. But Jesus came to die and pay the price for all our sins and break the power of sin and death. He died, but remember, He rose from the dead, victorious over sin, death, and hell."

Mariano turned away without a word. As time passed, he began to be more and more cruel to Russell. He took away the typewriter and broke it into pieces. He wouldn't let Russell have water, but just lemonade with drugs in it that made him feel sick and have nightmares. "I'll have to shoot you while you're asleep!" Mariano sneered. He stuck the point of his rifle right up to Russell's head.

Trying to reach out in kindness, Russell gave Mariano a gift from one of the packages his family had sent. "You kidnaped me as an act of terrorism," Russell said, "and to raise money to buy your weapons. But our loving and merciful God allowed it to happen, because He loves you and wants me to tell you all about Him. Christianity isn't a system like socialism or capitalism. It's a personal relationship with the true God through Jesus Christ."

At midnight, on New Year's Eve, a group of Russell's kidnapers boisterously sang to him. Then one of them whispered, "We know you don't really work for our enemies."

"How do you know?"

"You aren't afraid of us. All the others we've kidnaped have always been afraid of us, and we could break them down with the drugs and the threats and the mind control, but you're different. Besides, the farmers told us that you used your airplane to help people. The farmers all speak very highly of you."

The very next day, Russell received the word. "This is it!" some of his kidnapers yelled, as they took down his hammock. "You're going to be released!"

Several of them accompanied him to the dock where his brother, who had spent the last five months working out the ransom deal, waited for him.

For almost five months, Russell had lived in this camp, and now he thought of some of these men as friends. He shook hands with each one and gave him a hug. "Goodbye, friend," he said. "I hope we can meet again under better circumstances."

Mariano, who had hated him so deeply, who had treated him so terribly, began to cry. He grabbed Russell's hand and held it. Then he choked out, "Forgive me for the way I treated you. Forgive me."

"Don't think about it again," Russell answered as he hugged him. "Just remember the words I've said to you."

Russell climbed into the speedboat next to his brother. The boat sped away, and Russell waved to his kidnapers. They waved back.

They're in prison, O Lord, he thought. *Who will rescue them? When will they come to the full deliverance You offer through Jesus Christ?*

* * *

After Russell was released, he published the book he wrote when he was a captive in the revolutionary camp, calling it *Rescue the Captors*. Thousands of copies were given away all over the areas controlled by the revolutionaries. Many revolutionaries read it and eventually came to Christ. Some of them became pastors and Bible distributors, giving their lives for the Savior that they used to hate.

Six years later, Giovanni found Russell and gave him a message. "On behalf of the entire movement of the Revolutionary Armed Forces of Colombia," he said, "we apologize and ask forgiveness for kidnaping you. Everyone knows that it was a big mistake."

See Thinking Further for Chapter 9 on page 139.

10. SENDING OUT THE SIGNAL

The voice crackled on the radio. "My brother, Pablo Cortez, if you're alive, I hope you hear this message. Our family is doing okay, but we miss you."

Another voice came through the signal. "This message is for our daughter, Maria Fernandez. We think you're with the revolutionaries someplace, and we want you to know we love you, and we pray for you every night."

Around the area, hidden in their jungle camps, the revolutionaries held their small radios up to their ears and strained to listen. If there was a message for one of them, they didn't want to miss it.

By 1994, the terrible violence in Colombia had forced the last of the Wycliffe missionaries to fly away, but Russell Stendal stayed, with his wife and children. By 1999, with equipment and permission, Russell was able to start an evangelical radio station at the old mission base.

In between the messages from family members, Russell played lively Colombian music. And he spoke short messages of hope.

"There is hope for our war-torn land of Colombia. That hope is found in the love of Jesus Christ." Russell's voice became familiar to farmers, fisherman, and revolutionaries all over that part of Colombia. Month after month, year after year, they listened.

"Are you listening to that preacher again, Maria?" growled one of the revolutionaries. "That gringo that talks about love?" His voice dripped with sarcasm, and he shifted his machine gun over his shoulder. "We kill those weak Christians, you know. We burn those Bibles and other books. We can't have their lies in our country when our revolution frees Colombia!"

Quickly, Maria snapped off her small radio. "I heard a message from my father," she mumbled. "I meant to turn it off before that evangélico started talking." She flipped her hair behind her and lifted her chin. Then she took her crutch and hobbled to the other part of the cabin where her own radio equipment was set up. Even though she had lost her leg when she stepped on that land mine, that wouldn't stop her from serving the cause of the revolution.

Maria sat down before the microphone, and spoke smoothly. "Greetings, comrades," she said. "This is the

Voice of the Resistance. The voice of the freedom of Colombia!" She was a revolutionary, a communist, an atheist! Jesus Christ—He was weak, He had died! This was 2005—who believed in that old-fashioned idea of God in this modern day?

Even as she listened to her own voice, those other voices still echoed in her head. The voice of her old father—she might never see him again. The voice of that gringo, the one who talked about love and forgiveness—that weak man. She heard his voice again, even in her sleep. Sometimes, when no one noticed, she clicked her little battery-powered radio back on.

One day, as Maria sat at her radio controls in the corner of the cabin preparing for her next program, she heard a familiar voice in another part of the small building. It sounded … like that gringo evangélico. Even though she was the Voice of the Resistance, Maria had still listened to that other voice enough times to be pretty sure she could recognize it. She got up, and went around the corner to peek. Surely it was. He was blond—she had always pictured him as blond. Why was he here? Maria hobbled back to the corner with her radio equipment, where she felt safe.

Then Russell came into the room. "It's good to meet you," he said. "I see that you're in communication work too." He smiled.

"Yes," Maria murmured. She took the hand he offered, and her eyes darted toward him. "Why are you here?"

"Oh, I was meeting one of your leaders," Russell answered casually. "Where are you from?" She didn't know it, but he was looking for someone.

"From El Tigre," she responded, not looking up.

"Oh, I know a farmer from there. Do you know Pedro Fernandez?"

Before she could stop herself, Maria's eyes filled with tears. She put her hand over her mouth. "That's my father," she sobbed. "I wish I could contact my family."

"Maria," said Russell. "Your parents have asked me to find you if I could. Will you come home to them?"

Maria covered her face with her hands and shook her head. "I can't," she said. "If I leave here, they'll kill me. They kill anyone who leaves."

"I'll be praying for you," Russell said gently. "Your family prays for you every day. Here. This is a New Testament for you to read, along with some books. Here's your father's phone number. Keep listening to the words of hope on the radio—here's one that works on solar power. May I take a picture of you for your family?"

Maria sniffed and nodded and took the books and radio without another word.

Russell knew that Maria's life would be in danger if she left. He had known so many people—revolutionaries who had become Christians, even pastors—who were now dead because of their stand for Jesus Christ.

Maria didn't know it, but that photo went somewhere else besides her family. A copy of it went into the *Voice of the Martyrs* magazine, where thousands of Christians all over the world could see it and pray for her.

The people of the revolution had said they wanted to bring freedom for Colombia. Instead, they brought death, destruction, and terror.

On the radio, Russell preached words of hope, love and truth. He had spent seven years working on a new translation of the Bible for the people of Colombia, and now everything that he had received in his spirit came out in his words. He preached on the radio for hours and hours at a time.

"Jesus told the woman at the well that He is the Living Water. He gives to all who thirst," Russell preached. Farmers talked about it as they passed each other on the road.

"Paul said that when he was weak, then he was strong," Russell preached. Revolutionaries thought about it in the night, when their murders kept them from sleep.

What did it mean? How could they have this Living Water? How could they have this strength? Secretly or with their families, the people in that part of Colombia listened.

Hungry. Thirsty. Needy.

"Love and kindness from the living Lord of heaven—these are the ways to help our broken nation of Colombia," Russell's familiar voice sounded over the radio. His heart ached to see the nation that he loved be restored.

Was there really a God? Maria tossed on her small mattress. *Was Karl Marx, the founder of communism, really wrong?*

The voice on the radio said, "Jesus told us that you will know the truth and the truth will make you free!" That man's voice. That kind man. What had made her think he was weak?

Less than a year later, Russell received a call from a voice that sounded strangely familiar. "Who are you?" he asked.

"I can't tell you," said the voice, "but I have some people here who need to be safe from the killers. We want your help. Will you come?"

This happened often. A mysterious voice over the phone would ask Russell for help. Then he would come and find that it was someone he had prayed for, for maybe ten or fifteen years.

Or … maybe he would walk into a trap. He had to be led by the Spirit of God.

Russell asked his faithful God to lead him. Then, he answered, "Yes, I'll be there as soon as I can."

In the middle of the night, he drove through an area thick with bandits, kidnapers, revolutionaries, and other criminals. There, in the middle of the night, he found an almost abandoned store with several people huddled together. As many people as possible piled into his car, so he could drive them to safety.

Then, he drove back for the second time in order to get the rest of them. There, in the second group, stood Maria. "The soldiers attacked us, and I couldn't

run," she said, pointing to her wooden leg. "I hid in the bushes for three days, and then a friend helped me get down here."

Russell drove Maria and the others back to safety.

"I want to work for your radio station now," Maria declared boldly. "I believe in God—I believe in Jesus Christ! I know how to work on the radio, and I want to help."

* * *

Maria returned to her Christian family and changed teams. No longer was she the Voice of the Resistance, she had become one of the voices of truth. The revolutionaries heard her voice and wanted to kill her, but Russell and others protected her. Many generous Christians contributed to help Maria get a new artificial leg, and she continued to serve the cause of Jesus Christ.

See Thinking Further for Chapter 10 on page 140.

11. I WANT THAT MOUNTAIN

Year after year, Russell looked up at La Montaña. "Lord, I claim that mountain for You," he prayed. "If our radio station had a transmitter up there, think of how many more people we would reach with the words of truth!"

However, violent revolutionaries with machine guns had claimed the top of La Montaña. They stole cattle from the farmers—the very farmers they claimed they wanted to help—in order to feed their men. They kidnaped people to try to raise money to support themselves. Sometimes they killed them brutally.

At the bottom of La Montaña, surrounding the revolutionaries, were the paramilitary. Many years ago, they used to work for the real Colombian military. Now, they didn't obey the real military anymore—they just wanted to fight and kill all the revolutionaries ... and anyone who helped the revolutionaries ... and anyone who might have helped someone who helped the revolutionaries

... and the families of the people who might have helped the revolutionaries.

Everywhere around that ancient mountain, death and destruction reigned. People lived in constant fear for their lives.

Surely, it would be impossible to get a radio transmitter up there.

Russell didn't know it, but the revolutionary commander on top of La Montaña was desperate for help. He remembered meeting Russell years ago when Russell was trying to help some revolutionaries. Every day, he listened to Russell on the radio.

"Each one of us, in our own hearts, must turn to God for forgiveness through Christ," Russell preached. "Every one of us must repent."

Noel, the commander, didn't understand everything Russell preached about, but he knew the revolutionary way wasn't working. His people were starving, and he didn't know what to do. He felt trapped.

One day, Noel called Russell. Without revealing who he was, he said, "I need you to come to see us. I'll send someone to show you where."

The Holy Spirit gave Russell peace, and he answered the voice on the phone, "Yes, I'll meet you."

As Russell followed his guide through the jungle, he saw that they were heading up the very mountain he had been praying for. When he arrived at the top, he looked around at the revolutionaries who had lived up there, some of them for years and years, trying to survive by hunting and stealing cattle. They were prisoners of their own revolution.

"I pray for this mountain every time I pass by it," he told Noel. "I prayed for it long before I knew you were up here. Even when I was kidnaped and tied to a tree, I wanted to reach the revolutionaries for Christ. And now, here we are, you and me together. I know this is no coincidence in the plan of God."

"Look," said Noel, "all I know is that we need friends. My people starve, and we can't get any food because the filthy paramilitary guard the base of the mountain. However, I know we can trust you. I know you want to help us. I assure you that my friends will be your friends, and your friends will be welcome here. We need help."

Russell handed Noel a book, *Jesus, Friend of Terrorists*. "Do you think this would be a good book for the paramilitary?" he asked.

Noel looked at it. "It's perfect for those dirty dogs, those pigs," he growled. "They need a book like this. Maybe it will turn them around." He stuck it in his pocket. "They need that thing you always preach about called repentance."

"Listen, I've asked God for years to make a way for me to bring the voice of truth throughout Colombia," said Russell. "The only way to reach these people is through books like these, or through the radio, and if we put a radio transmitter up here, we can reach many, many more people."

"I want you to do that," Noel answered. "I want you to put that radio transmitter up here."

Russell went back down the mountain. He marveled at the door of opportunity which the Lord had opened with the revolutionaries.

The next day, the paramilitary captured Russell. "What were you doing up on La Montaña?" the commander demanded. He waved his machine gun in Russell's face. "We saw you up there!"

"Maybe you won't believe me," Russell answered. "However, the revolutionaries called me because they listen to my radio station. They want me to put a transmitter up there so they can hear it better, and so it can be broadcast to many more people. I gave them these books. Read this one and tell me if you think it's a good book for them."

The commander looked at the cover. "*Jesus, Friend of Terrorists*," he read. "This is good for them, for sure. Those dogs need that radio station. They need that thing you preach about called repentance."

"Maybe you could help me set up the equipment," Russell said. "Then they'll all be able to hear the radio station, and you can check up on what they hear."

Without delay, the paramilitary went to work to help Russell find a good location for the radio transmitter up the far side of the mountain. Many men went with him to help.

"Here," Russell said to the paramilitary men. "I have some books for you, and Bibles." He handed them book after book after book, even one about Karl Marx, the founder of communism. It was called *Marx and Satan*. "I have to be careful when I hand out this one," he said. "Sometimes, when the revolutionaries read it, they want to shoot me."

Before long, Noel called him again.

"Hello, friend," Noel said on the phone. "Will you bring me that man named Julian? I think he can help us." Noel was talking about a priest, but Russell thought he meant a commander of the paramilitary, their enemies.

Julian, the paramilitary leader, thought the revolutionaries were about to surrender.

Up the mountain they went. The paramilitary man felt confident. Russell felt nervous, but Noel thought Russell brought a priest! When he found out it was a paramilitary, he was furious and wanted to kill him.

Russell said, "Listen, Noel, we made a mistake. I don't know a priest named Julian. But don't you remember what you said? You said that my friends would always be welcome here, didn't you? This man, this paramilitary, is my friend. Maybe this was in the plan of God, for you to sit down and talk."

Finally, after decades of killing each other, a leader of the revolutionaries and a leader of the paramilitary sat down together. They glared at each other across the table.

"You've done terrible things!" yelled the paramilitary man. "You've murdered and destroyed! You killed my father!"

"You've done terrible things too!" yelled one of the revolutionaries. "Just as bad, or worse! You killed my family!"

"Listen," said Russell. "We've all done things that desperately need forgiveness. The only one who can give us that forgiveness is the Lord Jesus Christ. You can't change what has already happened. You can't do anything about what others are still doing, but you can change what's going on right here. Right now. Remember," he added, "the one who's been forgiven the most has the greatest capacity to love. And I'm not the one who said this. It was the Lord Jesus Christ."

The enemies continued to glare at each other across the table. All of them were silent.

"Listen," Russell said. "If a handful of people have destroyed this country, why can't a handful of people work together to restore it? You had a great heart for revenge. Why can't you have just as great a heart for love?"

Because Russell was there, the two sides listened—really listened—to each other's words.

When the paramilitary representative returned to his commander, he exclaimed, "I can't live with myself any longer! I want to leave the paramilitary."

"What do you mean, leave?" said his commander. "The punishment for that is death!"

The young man pounded the table. "How can we sow evil and reap good?" he cried out, echoing Russell's words. "How can we wipe out evil by causing more? How can we bring peace through war? How can we stop bloodshed by shedding blood?" He pointed to Russell. "I finally understand that this man is right. And we can choose to do right. We can choose to put our countrymen before our differences."

The commander looked at Russell. They all knew that the Spirit of God was on him.

"What do you suggest?" the commander finally asked.

"The revolutionaries are starving," answered the young paramilitary. "We have plenty of food. Let's do the right thing. Let's take some food up to them."

For a long time, the commander looked at the young man, and then looked at Russell. Eventually, he spoke.

"All right. We'll do that."

Before long, Russell led a team of mules and men up the mountain with a thousand pounds of food for the revolutionaries.

Like a vision in the twilight, the silhouettes appeared on the mountain. The revolutionaries saw that someone ... someone was climbing the mountain with mules laden with dozens of heavy packs.

The paramilitary had sent them food? How could this be?
Surely there must be a God.

With plenty of food, the revolutionaries soon stopped stealing the farmers' cattle.

The farmers were able to return to their farms.

After decades of war on La Montaña, there was peace, and the voice of peace sounded to all the countryside around.

"The weaker we are, the more glorious God's work in this nation can be through us." Russell's voice broadcast loud and clear

all hours of the day and night over the transmitter on top of La Montaña.

"Now is the time for the weak. Now is the time for Colombia."

* * *

In 2012, the story of *La Montaña* was made into a full-length movie by Russell's daughters, Lisa and Alethia. The Stendal family showed it to revolutionaries and paramilitary all throughout Colombia. Everywhere they showed it, men and women were stunned at the power of the love and forgiveness of the loving heavenly Father. Many gave their hearts to Jesus Christ.

See Thinking Further for Chapter 11 on page 140.

12. ANA AND THE DEMONS

Ana said, "I must have demons, Pastor Julio. I think about killing other people all the time. I want to kill myself, too. I can't have knives around me." She pulled her shawl around her shoulders and shivered. "When I go into the rages, everyone is terrified of me."

"Well," said Pastor Julio. "I've already tried all the prayers I know. I don't know any more words to say. So I have an idea. Here's what we'll do. Do you know the men out there who grow those huge fields of illegal drugs?" He waved his arm toward the west.

"Yes, of course," answered Ana. Everyone knew about those. The coca fields were very profitable for the growers, because those gringos from the U.S. always wanted the drugs. Some of the growers around the area were becoming very rich.

"Since you're not afraid to kill anyone, and since they're all terrified of you, you can go collect tithes for my church from those drug growers. Just tell them

them if they won't pay their tithes to the
can go when you're in one of your rages."
stood confused. Was this right? It didn't seem
right.

But what was right? The Jehovah's Witnesses had
told her that she had to obey their rules, but those rules
had brought her no peace. One preacher had cheated
her out of so much money she had lost her small store.
Another had told her she was under a curse because she
ate pork. What was right?

Ana walked away, dejected. Her mind began spinning,
and voices in her head spoke many strange things.
Which was right? Which was wrong?

One day, Pastor Julio gathered all the people from
all the surrounding area for a huge meeting. Ana stood
with her head down. She stared at the ground and
gripped her shawl around her shoulders. The pastor
began to preach.

"The reason you're poor is because you don't think
BIG!" Pastor Julio preached. "God wants to bless the
people who think BIG!" He began to strut up and
down in front of the crowd, many of whom were in
rags. "You see my suit?" he asked. "You know how I got
this? It's because I thought BIG! God doesn't want His
people to live in rags! God doesn't want His people

to eat beans! He wants them to wear expensive suits and eat steak! That's what God wants for His children! All you have to do is give and give until you can't give any more, and then God will bless you the same way. Remember that you're—"

What kinds of words were these? Suddenly, Ana screamed. A blood-curdling scream. A scream of fury, of murder. Around her, some other women screamed too.

"I'll kill you!" Ana screamed. She tore her shawl in half and clawed at the air, with fire in her eyes. "I'll kill you all! I'll tear you apart!" She began to rage through the crowd, waving her arms wildly, hitting people, tearing her clothes. She ran right through a barbed wire fence and fell on the ground, bleeding.

Finally, the police were able to capture Ana. They took her to a mental hospital where she sat tied up, her eyes glazed over.

"You know what your problem is?" the people there said. "You don't have a patron saint. You need to have a patron saint. And how many rosaries have you prayed to the Virgin? Not any? That's your problem! Pray rosaries, pray many times a day, and your problems will go away."

Ana began to pray rosaries to the Virgin. She sank into deep depression. She knew the demons hadn't left. Everything seemed to become black, and she felt as if her brain were rotting away.

But at least she was quiet now, and the people at the hospital sent her home.

"I'm still afraid I'll kill someone," she murmured to herself. "I don't want to leave a knife around." She sat down heavily in a chair on her small porch and began to cry. She tried to shut out the voices, but they still yelled inside her head. They yelled terrible things.

Ana watched the revolutionaries walk down the path, by her house, into the jungle. They avoided her gaze as they walked by—they were afraid of that crazy lady. Somewhere in that jungle was their secret camp. Her house was the last house where ordinary travelers were allowed to go. If they went any farther into the jungle, they could be shot.

"Hey, lady," a man called. "I've got something to sell. Something good."

Ana looked up, confused. What was it now? It didn't matter. She didn't have any money.

"Look," the man said. "It's a radio. And you can hear some pretty good music."

Ana looked at it. Suddenly she felt as if she had to have that radio. Maybe it was because she hoped it would turn her thoughts away from all those voices.

"Here," she said impulsively. "Will you take these two chickens for that radio?" It was a crazy thing to do. Those were two of her last chickens.

"Sure," said the man. "Sounds good." He took the chickens and walked away.

Ana found that the radio dial would turn to only one station. Only one. Strange.

But it was okay because it was good music, happy music. Maybe that music would help her forget her troubles.

Then a voice came on the radio. "God is real," the voice said. "He has a heart for Colombia. He loves our war-torn land and wants to redeem her. There is darkness here, but Jesus Christ, the living Son of God, is the Light of the world."

Ana suddenly became stiff with shock. She had never heard any words like these.

Over days and weeks, Ana listened and listened. She heard words of hope, words of love. She began to understand who Jesus Christ was. She even began to pray.

"Oh God," she prayed. "If You're real—I think You are—I want to meet that man who speaks on that radio. I need to ask him some questions."

One day, a stranger walked past the house. He was blond, a gringo. "Who is he?" thought Ana. "I've never seen him before." Something inside her compelled her to call out. "Hey! Mister! What are you doing here?" She had to hear his voice.

"I'm here to visit one of the revolutionaries," came the reply. That voice! She recognized that voice! Somehow she knew it would be that voice!

"I've got to talk to you!" Ana cried out. "I've got to talk to you."

"I'm so sorry," Russell replied ruefully. "I can't stay. I have to meet with the revolutionary leader named Eduardo. Listen, here's a radio for you; it runs on solar power and doesn't need any batteries."

"I have one of those already," Ana answered quietly, still staring at him. "I listen to your voice all the time. I want to talk to you."

"I'm so sorry," Russell said again. "I'll try to come back soon. But take the radio anyway and give it to someone else. And here are some books for you to read. This is a devotional book." It was a copy of *Extreme Devotion* by Voice of the Martyrs.

Ana took the book in her hands and struggled to find words. Something had suddenly happened. She felt as if the darkness had lifted. "Thank you. Thank you. Will you come back?"

"I'll come back."

God had answered her prayer! She had met the man on the radio! She listened to the radio even more and prayed for God to open her ears to hear His truth and deliver her. She read the books and

believed what she read and trusted Jesus Christ for her salvation.

"It's real! It's true!" Ana said to the revolutionaries and anyone else who came past her house. "Jesus has delivered me from the demons! I no longer hear the evil voices."

Every day, she watched for Russell's return. And one day, he arrived.

"I have to tell you what Jesus did for me!" Ana gasped out, her words tumbling over each other. "I'm free from the demons! I'm delivered!"

She told Russell her whole story. "And now, these people"—she waved her arm toward the jungle—"they're starting to listen to me. When the crazy lady invites them in for coffee and they see I'm not crazy, they think maybe this Jesus isn't as weak as they thought He was! Huh! It's like the stories I read in here." She held up the Bible. "Jesus cast the demons out of people. I didn't even know those stories before. But now He has done the same thing for me."

"Praise God," Russell began. "If you—"

"Now listen to me, I'm not finished," Ana continued. "This is what I want you to do. My house is right on the edge of the area controlled by the rebels, those revolutionaries. Past this house"—she pointed toward the small road—"past this house, they all go. The preachers, the farmers, the coca growers, the drug traffickers, the rebels. Sometimes even the regular army. They all come here. So you can put stacks and stacks of books and Bibles and radios in my house. Here, that looks like a good one." She picked up the one called *Marx and Satan.* "So he had demons too, eh? I'm not surprised."

"You'll be able to give away the Bibles and books I bring you?" Russell asked. "Will you be in danger?"

"Yes, I'll give them to everyone who comes here. It doesn't matter if I'm in danger. This is what I want to do. It's right. It's true. And listen, they all want them—they all read them. They all have questions I can't answer, so I just tell them, you keep listening to *that*"—she pointed to the radio—"and you keep reading *that*"—she pointed to the Bible—"and you'll get your questions answered. I didn't tell them that maybe the radio man would come by sometime to answer some of their questions." She chuckled.

Russell brought stacks of books and Bibles to Ana's house. Every time he returned, he brought more. The revolutionaries, the coca growers, the coffee farmers, the military, the drug dealers, all of them wanted the books and Bibles from the lady who used to be crazy— but was now in her right mind.

They began to come to Christ. Even Eduardo, the revolutionary leader Russell was meeting with, became a strong believer. Coca growers left the fields. Drug traffickers left their illegal work. These men became pastors who preached the true message of salvation and power through Jesus Christ.

They began to pass out the radios, the Bibles, the books, to everyone they knew. With people like these, it was hard for Russell to keep enough books, Bibles, and radios on hand.

* * *

In 2006, God provided Russell with an airplane to spread the gospel. Voice of the Martyrs and other mission organizations helped provide him with small parachutes filled with Bibles, books, and radios that they called 'Truth Packs.' These he could drop over places where he never could have traveled on land. More and more revolutionaries began to hear the gospel of Jesus Christ.

See Thinking Further for Chapter 12 on page 141.

13. A "BEAUTIFUL VIEW" FROM THE JAWS OF HELL

Oscar Osorio held up his copy of the newspaper. "Jeannine, you wanted this story, right?" The headline shouted, "One Year in Bellavista No Deaths!" Bellavista was the notoriously violent prison in Medellín that people called the Jaws of Hell.

Bellavista—the name meant "beautiful view." But even though Medellín did have a beautiful view of the majestic mountains, it seemed that the drug lords ruled the whole city. Killing was a way of life. Before this year, in that prison, there had been between thirty and sixty murders every month.

But now ...

"Yes, I saw it," Jeannine Brabon replied. "It seems almost unbelievable for a secular newspaper to talk this way about how Jesus has changed lives." Before she was born, her missionary parents had been warned by this same newspaper, "By blood or by fire we will drive the Protestants out." To think that now they were saying that Jesus was the answer to the violence!

The only explanation was the power of God to change a culture.

"I want you to come to the prison with me," Oscar said. "Let's go early tomorrow morning!"

Eagerly, Jeannine agreed. She didn't know what was in store, but she wanted to go wherever the Lord would lead her.

The next morning, as they moved through the crowded street, Oscar scanned his eyes along the ridge of the huge mountains towering over the city, where he knew so many revolutionaries, drug growers, and other criminals lived. He had been one of those. He had been a criminal.

"Last year, a year ago, it was bad, really bad." Oscar shook his head, recalling the memories of those horrible days. "The prison guards walked away. They just walked away. They couldn't take it anymore. All the killing and the blood." He held up his hands and looked at them, as if they were covered with blood. "They were about to call the army into the prison to stop the rioting and killing! Something had to happen.

"So I went and talked to the director of the prison. I told him that the Lord changed me and he was the same Lord who had the power to change any man. Then he said I could go in every day.

"I called on my friends to pray," Oscar continued. "We prayed. We wanted to be people of peace. So we went into that prison and asked the men to lift white flags—the sign of peace, you know."

Jeannine nodded. White flags were the sign of surrender. Helplessness. Weakness.

"We didn't know what those wild men would do. Most of them were imprisoned for murder, you know. They went in for murder, and then they committed more murders when they were there." He shook his head again at the sadness of it all, and studied his hands. Did they have blood on them?

"We walked in like an army, in a way," Oscar said. "But we were an army with no weapons except the Word of God and prayer. And faith. We had faith that if we lived or died, we would be safe in the arms of our loving Father."

Jeannine gazed off into the distance, to the brilliant Colombian sky above the drab and crowded city. She listened.

"I went to the microphone," Oscar continued, "to speak to all the prisoners. Those prisoners, they looked so angry, they had a kind of devil fire in their eyes, you know. Yet each one of the men took a tiny white flag made on a toothpick. We played the national anthem and I asked them to lift up their flags, and they did!

"I looked over all of them, and you know the feeling I felt inside of me?" Oscar made a motion with his hands as if he could gather up all his feelings inside of him.

"It probably wasn't fear, was it?" Jeannine asked.

"No, it wasn't fear. I felt compassion. I felt so much compassion that I thought I would burst with the love of Jesus Christ for them. I began to cry. I knew that the worst prison was not this place; this hell-hole, this prison that was holding four times as many men as it was supposed to. The worst prison was inside themselves, just the way it was for me before I met Jesus.

"So I preached to them. I didn't know if they would try to rush on us and kill us all. But I preached to them about their sin and their need to repent and turn to Christ.

"And Jeannine." Oscar turned to her. "They began to weep. They began to lay down their weapons. They began to go down on their knees. Do you know what happened?"

"The Holy Spirit came down in the prison," Jeannine murmured.

"That's exactly it. The Holy Spirit, like a flame of fire, came down in that prison. So for a year I've led the meetings, and they've grown larger and larger. But Jeannine, I'm really tired. So I want to ask you if you'll speak this morning."

They had almost arrived at Bellavista. The prison loomed before them, huge and cold and gray, surrounded by walls twelve feet high, surrounded by guards posted with guns. "You want me to speak?" Jeannine asked. Was this the opportunity she was praying for, to stand against the culture of death?

"Yes, I'm sure the Holy Spirit has a good word for you to say."

"Who do you expect to come to the meeting?"

"A lot of men always come. New believers and unbelievers. Most of them are in for murder. They're in for life ... or death."

Instead of fear, Jeannine felt her heart fill up with love. Love for Christ and love for the murderers. God's perfect love cast out her fear. "Lord, what do you want me to say to them?" she murmured. "I want You to be the one that's lifted up."

Immediately, the story of David and Mephibosheth came into her mind.

When they arrived, Jeannine stood at the podium before a room full of young men. Some of them knew Jesus and were eager to hear her. Some of them were curious, searching. Some of them were scoffers.

So she began to speak.

"David was a powerful king. The kind of king who could wipe out all his enemies with a single command if he wanted to."

A murmur went through the crowd. Some of them wanted power like that.

"David feared God. He knew that, in the power of God, a powerful man could still be kind and good. He had made a commitment of kindness to help any sons of his friend, Jonathan. It just so happened that Mephibosheth would also be the grandson of his mortal enemy, King Saul. King Saul was the one who had hunted David for years and years, who wanted to kill him."

The men leaned forward, interested to hear how such a predicament would play out. They had known what it was like to hunt another man. And to be hunted.

"That young man was lame," Jeannine continued. "It would have been very easy for David to kill him. No one would have blamed him. Almost nobody would have even cared. But that isn't what David did.

"Instead, David brought that lame man to his own home and treated him like his own son. He treated him with love and compassion. He even let him eat at the king's table.

"This is what Jesus does for us. We are the children of the enemy. Our hands are covered with blood. But Jesus says, 'I will bring you into My family. You will be My own son. You can eat at My table.' Jesus says, 'Come.' "

When Jeannine finished, she watched with astonishment as twenty young men stood up with tears running down their faces. "We want Jesus!" they said. Some of these young men used to be hired killers who would earn thousands of dollars for each murder. But now they said, "Please teach us. Show us how to live for Jesus by the power of the Holy Spirit. Teach us how to pray."

Because of those young men and many others, Jeannine asked her Bible seminary if she could start a Bible institute in the prison.

"Start a Bible institute in Bellavista?" the professors exclaimed. "It's the most dangerous prison in Latin America!"

"It used to be," Jeannine answered quietly. "But you should see what I've seen. More and more of them are coming to Christ. They meet for prayer and Bible study. They just need to be taught. Oscar can't really teach them—he's never even been trained himself. They need to be taught the Bible. They used to be leaders in crime, but they can become leaders in the churches."

Jeannine began to teach in the prison in 1991. Over twenty years later, she said to a friend, "Did you know that there has been an average of less than one murder a year in this place since then? It's crowded with revolutionaries and paramilitary and corrupt military and common criminals. Over seven thousand prisoners in a prison built for fifteen hundred. All of them come in hating each other, and then they have to sleep on the floor crowded next to the very men that they hate! But in this prison, they've been transformed by the power of Jesus Christ."

One young man, a student at the Biblical Seminary of Colombia, chose to do some of his practical work at Bellavista. Alex Puerta came in and told his story. "The revolutionaries killed everyone on my bus, all twenty-seven," he said. "I don't know why they did it, but they did." A hush of silence fell over the room as he touched the eye patch over his eye. "I was the only one that survived. That was the morning of September 20, 1995, nine years ago."

Alex didn't realize that the date and other information made one of the prisoners gasp. This was one of the revolutionaries who had stopped that bus and killed those people. He looked at his hands. Were they covered with blood?

"I knew I was about to die," Alex continued, "and I began to call out to them that Christ loves them. Then God told me to be quiet and seek life. I did that by pretending to be dead." He paused. "The revolutionaries left, thinking they had killed everyone. But I'm here today because God spared my life so I could tell you about His love and forgiveness. When Jesus died, He forgave me. Now I have His new life inside me, and I also forgive. The men who did this to us were ignorant. They didn't know about the new life Jesus offers."

A few minutes later, Alex received a whispered message. "One of those men is here," his friend said. "One of the murderers that you told about. He's afraid of you."

Alex's heart filled with compassion. "Please tell him that I really meant what I said," he whispered back. "Tell him that I forgive him."

It wasn't long before several men in the crowd were weeping, top leaders of the revolutionary forces. "We've always been told that Christians were weak," one of them said. "But we have never seen such strength as yours."

More and more of the men came to Christ every day. They rose early in the morning for prayer and Bible reading, and encouraged each other. They prayed all night with each other. They fasted, begging the Lord to continue His work in the prison. Even though only ten percent of them became evangélicos, somehow that ten percent changed the whole place. When their families came to visit on the weekends, they couldn't wait to tell them more about Jesus. The families were changed too.

These men—their hands had been covered with blood. But now, they raised them in the air and sang praises to their Savior, the One whose blood washes white as snow. They knew that their hands were clean, clean, clean, by the blood of the Lamb of God.

Inside the prison walls of Bellavista, these men saw the beautiful view of the Lamb of God who died for them, who rose for them. Inside the Jaws of Hell, they saw the beautiful view of the Kingdom of God.

See Thinking Further for Chapter 13 on page 141.

14. A NEW DAY IN COLOMBIA

In Colombia, the violence was growing. In Colombia, the Spirit of God was moving.

In Cali, the second largest city of Colombia, the mayor declared in 1996, "Jesus is Lord of Cali!" But the violence, the immorality, the drug wars, the kidnapings, the killing, the terrible sins didn't stop.

That same year, some Colombian Christians gathered and drove around that big city, all the way around. As they drove, they prayed for Jesus to capture Cali for Himself. They drove around it seven times. They prayed and prayed, claiming all that territory for Christ.

In August of 1999, four hundred Colombian pastors came together, preparing for the biggest prayer meeting Cali had ever known. They asked forgiveness of one another and from the Lord. They hugged each other and promised that their unity in God's great salvation, by grace alone, through faith alone, in Christ alone, would overcome all their differences.

And during that week, in Colombia, more and more murders took place. Even teenagers killed people.

"We can't guarantee your safety for this prayer meeting in that stadium," said the Cali police. "You'd better call it off."

"We can't call it off," said the mayor. "We must pray."

The next week, the big prayer meeting began. The Colombian Christians had rented out the huge stadium, and over three thousand people came to pray. They came from all over the world, to pray for the broken nation of Colombia.

And while they prayed, criminals all over the nation kidnaped anyone who seemed like they might have some money. They sold them to the revolutionaries, who kept them for ransom or maybe killed them.

The Christians prayed in that stadium. They prayed all night. They kept praying. More Christians began to join them. And more. And more.

Two nights later, the stadium—that stadium that could hold 35,000 people—overflowed, so that people had to stand outside, waiting for some to leave so that they could enter. And pray.

Outside somewhere, the drug lords made deals with the revolutionaries. They paid off the judges and the lawmakers and the police to let them sell their drugs.

"Just turn your eyes the other way when we drive by. Here's a million pesos."

Pray. Pray for our broken nation of Colombia.

And people in that stadium fell on their faces and wept. They wept over their own sin, the sins of their families, the sins of their city, and the sins of their nation.

"We will see a new day in Colombia," one speaker declared. "Our Father in heaven will bring us a new day. The Spirit of God will sweep over this nation with His great salvation through Jesus Christ."

And somewhere in Colombia, a hopeless murderer, who sits in a prison, looks up to see a new prisoner who has been transferred from Bellavista. That new man has a look of joy on his face, like that murderer has never seen.

Pray. Pray for our broken nation of Colombia.

And somewhere in the U.S., a family works to make small parachutes for Russell Stendal's Truth Pack drops. And prays.

And somewhere in the jungles, a revolutionary picks up a Truth Pack one of the missionaries has dropped from his airplane. He opens the first Bible he has ever held.

And the families of evangélicos, who have been killed, determine they will forgive. And love. And pray.

And missionaries and national believers who have labored long years with small churches continue to labor faithfully. And love. And pray.

And sparks of light fly throughout the nation. And beams of light shine across the land.

O mighty Lord of heaven, You have given a great salvation through Jesus Christ. We are the weak. You are strong. We are seeing a new day in Colombia.

See Thinking Further for Chapter 14 on page 142.

A MESSAGE FROM THE AUTHOR

All my life, everything I had ever heard about Colombia, South America, was frightening. I heard that Colombians were always killing each other, that they raised and sold more illegal drugs there than any place in the world, that people lived in constant fear of their lives. When I thought of Colombia, I thought of revolutionaries in camouflage uniforms with machine guns; I thought of violence, of destruction, of terror.

In the past few years, through the Voice of the Martyrs, I had heard that God was opening new doors in Colombia, even with those very men in camouflage uniforms and machine guns. I became excited about participating in the parachute project for Truth Packs. I heard from short-term mission leaders that certain parts of Colombia now actually welcomed American Christians with excitement, to come and give them the gospel.

Then, in January of 2013, I heard Russell Stendal speak at a Voice of the Martyrs conference. The amazing things he told us about what God is doing in Colombia led me on the path of research ... and a book.

Was I right in my assessment of Colombia? Completely, and it was even worse than I had imagined. But what I saw, as I researched, were real people, with loved ones and hopes and miseries, delivered from darkness, and then counting their lives as small lights that they wanted to shine like lasers for the advancing of the Kingdom of God and the delivering of souls and the crushing of the enemy in a cosmic battle. Some of them, God preserved miraculously time and time again. Some of them, though, were gruesomely killed in a moment of terrible violence. But if those lights were snuffed out, without fail more arose in their stead. I watched the blood of the martyrs spill on the hard soil of the rocky mountains of Colombia to then grow as the seed of the church.

My prayer is that one of the real people in this book, that you've never heard of before, will now stand to you as a hero of the Christian faith. I pray that these stories will show you, even more clearly, the terrible schemes of the Enemy of God, the eternal value of the Kingdom of God, the awesome power of the love of God, and the desperate need of those in darkness.

If this comes to pass, then my desire and goal for this book has been accomplished.

ABOUT THE MISSIONARIES
AND THE EVANGELICOS

Chapter 1: Let's Get Started
Jack, John and Rachel came to Colombia with a mission organization called World Evangelization Crusade, founded by C.T. Studd. The stories of their work in Colombia, along with that of several others, can be found in the books *Modern Crusaders: The Challenge of Colombia,* and *Mountain Movers.*

Elof Anderson and his wife, Isabel, went as missionaries to Colombia in 1937 with The Scandinavian Alliance Mission, which later became The Evangelical Alliance Mission (T.E.A.M.). Elof wrote the book *Hacaritama* about his work in Colombia, but the story recounted in chapter 1 was told to me by his son, Timothy, who was born in Colombia and has served there all his life.

Chapters 2-4: Rosa and the Christ Statue; Marco and the Burning House; and *José and the Demons*
These stories are found in the books by Isabel Anderson (wife of Elof), *Counted Worthy* and *Tried in the Fire.* Those

books are called fiction, but Isabel's son, Timothy, assured me that they are fiction only in the sense that the names have been changed. Martha Wall wrote these stories and others as non-fiction in the books *As a Roaring Lion* and *In Crossfire of Hate*.

Chapter 5: Victor and the Dream Hut
David Howard (who happens to be the brother of Elisabeth Elliot, wife of martyred missionary Jim Elliot) served as a director of mission work in Colombia from 1958 to 1967. These stories are taken from his book *Hammered as Gold* (later renamed *The Costly Harvest*), but more stories about the hidden hero, Victor Landero, can be found in *The Victor: The Victor Landero Story*, as told to Bob Owen.

Chapters 6-7: Russell and the Picture Book; and "I Make the Sun Rise"
Chad and Pat Stendal went to Colombia as missionaries with Wycliffe Bible Translators in 1964. These stories are in Chad's books *High Adventures in Colombia* and *Walking in the Spirit in Colombia*.

Chapters 8-9: Machine Guns and a Typewriter; and Rescue the Kidnapers
After Russell Stendal grew up with his siblings among the Kogi Indians, he later began to serve the Colombian farmers

through a fishing business. This story is taken from the book he wrote while he was kidnaped, *Rescue the Captors.*

Chapters 10-11: Sending Out the Signal; and I Want That Mountain

Russell Stendal later wrote the book *Rescue the Captors 2,* from which these stories are taken. In 2012, Russell Stendal's daughters, Lisa and Alethia, published a video they had made, telling the true story of *La Montaña,* the source of the story in this chapter. Because of rough language and other factors, I wouldn't recommend the video for children, but the story it tells is a powerful one of love and forgiveness. (Russell is called Martín throughout the video because that's his middle name, and it's the name by which he's known in Colombia.) The narrated introduction to the video is so beautiful that I'm quoting it on page 134.

Chapter 12: Ana and the Demons

This story is taken from Russell Stendal's newsletter of September 2011.

Chapter 13: A "Beautiful View" from the Jaws of Hell

The story of Bellavista prison is recounted in several sources available on the internet, and is detailed in the book *The Lord of Bellavista* by David Miller.

Chapter 14: A New Day in Colombia

The story of the Cali prayer meetings is available from a number of sources on the internet.

If you and your family might be interested in making simple parachutes for Truth Pack drops for Colombia, you can visit the Voice of the Martyrs website to learn more about it.

FROM THE INTRODUCTION TO LA MONTAÑA

In the countryside of Colombia, people scream.
They flee, displaced from their lands.
Foreigners fear our country.
Even we are afraid.
This is our Colombia, but God came to free her.

In this final hour, I've asked God
Why He has left us for the last.
The Lord loves our country.
He says we are the last because we are the weakest.

He has sent the strong ahead.
The Lord raised up men like Abel and Abraham
And hired them at six in the morning.
He chose kings like David
And prophets like Isaiah and Nehemiah
And hired them at nine.
At noon He hired men like the apostles Peter and Paul.
In the afternoon he hired missionaries
Like Americans and Englishmen
That have spread His Word around the world.

And now at the end of this great day of humanity,
He hires us
Who are the weakest
Because He comes to show His power.

THINKING FURTHER

CHAPTER 1 – LET'S GET STARTED

"This Jesus is the stone that was rejected by you, the builders, which has become the cornerstone. And there is salvation in no one else, for there is no other name under heaven given among men by which we must be saved" Acts 4:11-12.

What did Jack mean when he prayed that God would open the peoples' "blind eyes"? What would the people see when their eyes were opened?

What did the jailer mean when he said, "Murderers get three years"? How important does the crime of murder seem to have been in Colombia?

How can a person try to work his way to God? Why is this a hopeless way?

CHAPTER 2 – ROSA AND THE CHRIST STATUE

"Their idols are silver and gold, the work of human hands. They have mouths, but do not speak; eyes, but do not see. They have ears, but do not hear; noses, but do not smell. They have hands, but do not feel; feet, but do not walk; and they do not make a sound in their throat" Psalm 115: 4-7.

Why were Rosa and her family so shocked to hear that the other word for "good news" was evangelio?

Why do you suppose the priests were so afraid of the *evangelio*?

Why did Marco turn away from his nephews and refuse to listen to them any more?

Purgatory is taught in some religions as a place of fire where people will pay for their sins after death before they can go to heaven. Why would Jesus' perfect sacrifice mean that no purgatory would be necessary?

What conflict did Rosa feel in her heart about trusting in Jesus Christ? How did that conflict finally end?

CHAPTER 3 – MARCO AND THE BURNING HOUSE

"You have heard that it was said, 'You shall love your neighbor and hate your enemy.' But I say to you, Love your enemies and pray for those who persecute you, so that you may be sons of your Father who is in heaven" Matthew 5:43-45.

Why wouldn't Marco and Vicente protect themselves from their attackers? Whose example were they following?

What was wrong with Marco to make him lie in bed for days and weeks, crying?

How did Pastor Vicente help Marco recover?

How did God rescue the family from the burning house?

God had rescued the family, and the family refused to hate their enemies. Which of these made more difference to the people of the village? What was the result?

CHAPTER 4 - JOSÉ AND THE DEMONS

"He has delivered us from the domain of darkness and transferred us to the kingdom of his beloved Son, in whom we have redemption, the forgiveness of sins" Colossians 1:13-14.

How did José bring darkness upon himself?

What did the Good News of Mark show José that he hadn't known before?

José still wanted power and decided to become an evangélico so he could get it. Why didn't his decision work?

How did José finally find freedom from the dark forces?

CHAPTER 5 - VICTOR AND THE DREAM HUT

"And a vision appeared to Paul in the night: a man of Macedonia was standing there, urging him and saying, "Come over to Macedonia and help us" Acts 16:9.

Describe the two dreams in this chapter. How did God make the dreams connect?

How did God prepare not only the heart of the woman who had the dream, but also all the people in the surrounding homes?

Victor Landero saw thousands of souls come to Christ in Colombia. Why did he then work among the Indians who had no interest in the gospel?

CHAPTER 6 – RUSSELL AND THE PICTURE BOOK

"How then will they call on him in whom they have not believed? And how are they to believe in him of whom they have never heard? And how are they to hear without someone preaching?" Romans 10:14

Describe the story in the picture book that made Russell get so upset.

Why did the tribal family live that way?

Describe how God worked in the Stendal family.

What strange coincidence happened after the Stendals had connected with the Kogi people?

CHAPTER 7 – "I MAKE THE SUN RISE"

"The God of Abraham, the God of Isaac, and the God of Jacob, the God of our fathers, glorified his servant Jesus ... And his name— by faith in his name—has made this man strong whom you see and know, and the faith that is through Jesus has given the man this perfect health in the presence of you all" Acts 3:13, 16.

Why were most of the Kogis so fearful of outsiders?

Describe the spiritual darkness of the Kogi people.

Why was Chad cautious about the decision to go to the Mamarango tribe?

How did God use Chief Nacio's sickness to bring the gospel to the tribe? Describe the miracle God worked.

CHAPTER 8 - MACHINE GUNS AND A TYPEWRITER

"Do not be deceived: God is not mocked, for whatever one sows, that will he also reap. For the one who sows to his own flesh will from the flesh reap corruption, but the one who sows to the Spirit will from the Spirit reap eternal life. And let us not grow weary of doing good, for in due season we will reap, if we do not give up" Galatians 6:7-9.

What did Russell do wrong when he was kidnaped that he was sorry for later?

When he admitted that he did something wrong, how did this affect his kidnapers?

How did God use the book Russell was writing in the lives of the kidnapers?

Saying you believe one thing but living as if you believe another is called *hypocrisy*. What did Russell point out as hypocrisy in the lives of the revolutionaries?

CHAPTER 9 - RESCUE THE KIDNAPERS

"And do not fear those who kill the body but cannot kill the soul. Rather fear him who can destroy both soul and body in hell" Matthew 10:28.

What was the practical joke that Russell played on some of his kidnapers?

Why did the kidnapers hate the story of Jesus' death? What was it they didn't understand about it?

What were some of the things about Russell that helped the kidnapers know he really was who he claimed to be?

CHAPTER 10 - SENDING OUT THE SIGNAL

"For nothing is hidden except to be made manifest; nor is anything secret except to come to light. If anyone has ears to hear, let him hear. And he said to them, Pay attention to what you hear" Mark 4:22-24.

What did Maria think about Jesus that made her feel foolish for listening to the Christian radio?

Karl Marx, the founder of communism, taught that all religion was false. What did the revolutionaries believe Christian missionaries were trying to do with their teachings?

Why did Maria keep being drawn to listen to the Christian radio station?

How was it that people all over the world found out about Maria and began praying for her?

How did God finally rescue Maria?

CHAPTER 11 - I WANT THAT MOUNTAIN

Jesus said, *"This is my commandment, that you love one another as I have loved you. Greater love has no one than this, that someone lay down his life for his friends. You are my friends if you do what I command you. No longer do I call you servants, for the servant does not know what his master is doing; but I have called you friends, for all that I have heard from my Father I have made known to you" John 15:12-15.*

What did Russell want to do at the top of La Montaña?

Describe the two groups, one at the top of the mountain, and the other at the bottom of the mountain. How were they similar?

How did God bring peace to La Montaña?

CHAPTER 12 - ANA AND THE DEMONS

"Submit yourselves therefore to God. Resist the devil, and he will flee from you. Draw near to God, and he will draw near to you" James 4:7-8.

What did Pastor Julio teach that was wrong?

What were some of the ways that people tried to solve the problem of Ana's demons?

How did God answer Ana's prayer?

What did Ana start doing after she was delivered from the demons?

CHAPTER 13 - A "BEAUTIFUL VIEW" FROM THE JAWS OF HELL

"Christ loved the church and gave himself up for her, that he might sanctify her, having cleansed her by the washing of water with the

word, so that he might present the church to himself in splendor, without spot or wrinkle or any such thing, that she might be holy and without blemish" Ephesians 5:25b-27.

Tell the story of what the Lord did when Oscar preached to the men in the prison a year earlier.

Why was the story of David and Mephibosheth a good story for these prisoners to hear?

What strange coincidence happened when Alex, the man who almost died, gave his testimony in the prison?

What was it about the Christians that seemed so strong to the prisoners?

CHAPTER 14 - A NEW DAY IN COLOMBIA

"Praying at all times in the Spirit, with all prayer and supplication. To that end keep alert with all perseverance, making supplication for all the saints" Ephesians 6:18.

This is a chapter of contrasts. What are some of the good and bad things that were happening at the same time in Colombia?

What are some ways that God is still at work in the nation of Colombia?

OTHER BOOKS IN THE HIDDEN HEROES SERIES

Hidden Heroes 1: *With Two Hands:*
Stories of God at Work in Ethiopia
ISBN: 978-1-84550-539-4

Hidden Heroes 2: *The Good News Must Go Out:*
Stories of God at Work in the Central African Republic
ISBN: 978-1-84550-628-5

Hidden Heroes 3: *Witness Men:*
True Stories of God at Work in Papua, Indonesia
ISBN: 978-1-78191-515-8

Hidden Heroes 4: *Return of the White Book:*
True Stories of God at Work in Southeast Asia
ISBN: 978-1-78191-292-8

To access more information and activities about
Lights in a Dark Place, see the Christian Focus
website at www.christianfocus.com

CHRISTIAN FOCUS PUBLICATIONS

Christian Focus   Christian Heritage   CF4K   Mentor

Christian Focus Publications publishes books for adults and children under its four main imprints: Christian Focus, CF4K, Mentor and Christian Heritage. Our books reflect our conviction that God's Word is reliable and Jesus is the way to know him, and live for ever with him.

Our children's publication list includes a Sunday School curriculum that covers pre-school to early teens, and puzzle and activity books. We also publish personal and family devotional titles, biographies and inspirational stories that children will love.

If you are looking for quality Bible teaching for children then we have an excellent range of Bible stories and age-specific theological books.

From pre-school board books to teenage apologetics, we have it covered!

Find us at our web page: www.christianfocus.com